D1464601

1

Think Like Sherlock Holmes:
Creatively Solve Problems, Think with Clarity, Make Insightful Observations & Deductions, and Develop Quick & Accurate Instincts

By Peter Hollins,
Author and Researcher at
petehollins.com

Table of Contents

Table of Contents 5

Chapter 1. Think Like Sherlock Holmes. 7

Chapter 2. Thinking Outside The Box .. 29

Chapter 3. Observations and Deductive Reasoning 93

Chapter 4. Shift Your Perspective....... 147

Chapter 5. Think Critically 195

Summary Guide 221

Chapter 1. Think Like Sherlock Holmes

There is no individual person—real or fictional—who embodies problem-solving ability as much as Sherlock Holmes. The famous detective has gone through various interpretations, but do you know where he got his start?

Sir Arthur Conan Doyle created the British detective in 1887 in the story *A Study in Scarlet*. Doyle used the character of Holmes in a total of 60 adventures (four novels and 56 short stories). He was immediately popular and remains so to this day. Holmes has been portrayed in film and on television over 250 times, more than any other human literary character in history. (If not for the nonhuman Dracula, he'd be the most portrayed literary character, period.) Holmes remains massively popular, even in modern updates of the character in TV series like the BBC's *Sherlock* and CBS's *Elementary.*

Why are audiences still so riveted by Sherlock Holmes? Is it the devilishly charming hat and smoking pipe he is usually portrayed with? No, it's primarily because he makes solving complex problems look extraordinarily easy. He's the superhero genius we all wish we could be.

He's almost superhuman in how he can unravel a situation or person with what appears to be a small amount of information or data. His genius looks automatic, and his explanations of his thought processes make previously unanswerable questions look embarrassingly simple.

Holmes reveals how observation, critical thinking, and reasoning triumph in problem-solving. The amazing way he was written to be a crime-fighting force that was at once flawed and yet a genius made him relatable and made us think "I can do that as well!" This book aims to describe some ways you can adapt some of his techniques to solving problems in your own personal life.

Doyle created Sherlock Holmes as someone whose intelligence is off the charts and for whom problem-solving is nearly automatic. In essence, he saw connections and patterns because of his vast repository of knowledge. That's in part because he was the epiphany of a polymath—one who is an expert in a multitude of fields. Nobody can simply brush up on his methods and expect to become him—it's impossible. You yourself might notice if something was amiss while observing your favorite hobby—imagine having that same kind of acumen across all disciplines you come across.

But there are several ways Holmes can teach us how to improve real-life problem-solving by increasing our awareness and technique. Even if we don't possess Holmes's deep intelligence, we can enhance our own skills in finding patterns and almost immediately bettering our thought processes. This book will probe how Holmes thinks, reasons, and discovers the truth and how you can adapt and shape that knack to solve your own everyday mysteries.

Who Is Sherlock Holmes and What Makes Him a Genius?

Sherlock Holmes is a private detective-for-hire in London. Because of his renown super-genius, he's often sought out by local police detectives (most famously Inspector Lestrade) to help them with cases where they've hit a brick wall. He's a brain mercenary, in a sense. Dr. John Watson is Holmes's companion, who accompanies Holmes on most of his expeditions and tells the stories in Doyle's books.

There is no case Holmes can't solve. He explains the solutions so articulately and plainly that it makes those watching him feel almost stupid for not noticing the clues in the first place. But what specifically makes Holmes such a unique genius? Let's dive into his bibliography and get acquainted with some of his most revelatory acts of creative thinking and deduction. At the end, you might notice a few common themes that we can attempt to emulate for ourselves—probably not up to Sherlock's standard, but more than sufficient for our purposes!

Master of ciphers. Sherlock Holmes is an expert codebreaker, someone who analyzes messages written in alternative words, numbers, symbols, or patterns to keep their content secret to all those who don't know the code. Years of study and experience have enabled him to determine patterns and communication tricks criminals use to set forth their nefarious plans, and he stops them from causing more trouble than they already have.

Holmes has even written a monograph—a heavily detailed, written study of a single subject—in which he dissects and explains 160 entirely different ciphers. That is a *lot* of time spent hunkered over nonsense syllables and symbols.

In "The Adventure of the Dancing Men," Holmes cracks a hieroglyphic code that uses pictures of matchstick men in various positions to send some message. He uses a method called "frequency analysis," inspired by Edgar Allen Poe's tale "The Gold Bug." Holmes determines that each man in the hieroglyphic note represents a single alphabet character. Knowing that the most-used letter in the English alphabet is "e"— and reasoning that Elsie, the receiver of the note, is probably addressed by name somewhere in it—Holmes decodes the message in two hours and solves the case.

A younger Holmes also triumphs over cryptography in "The Adventure of the Gloria Scott." After reading a seemingly meaningless letter, Holmes deduces that the *real* message the sender intends to say is in every third word in the text—a method used in the real world by Civil War spies. In *The Valley of Fear*, the final Holmes novel, the detective cracks a book cipher in which the numbers in the message refer to pages and words in a published book.

This trick was used by Benedict Arnold in the Revolutionary War and Abner Doubleday in the Civil War. Of course, none of these triumphs would be possible unless you were the same freak of nature as Sherlock and happened to pen your PhD thesis on ciphers and codebreaking. How convenient for him—less so for us!

Expert in footprints, forensics, and tracking. About half of all Sherlock Holmes stories contain some evidence gleaned from footprints, and Holmes was all over it. The very first Holmes story, *A Study in Scarlet,* describes footprints on "clayey soil." "The Adventure of the Lion's Mane" contains a long passage describing the detective following footsteps.

"The Boscombe Valley Mystery" takes Holmes's footprint expertise to almost ridiculous lengths, using only footprint evidence to solve the case. After taking close inspection of footprints on the ground at the scene of a crime, Holmes informs Lestrade, "The murderer is a tall man, left-handed, limps with the right leg, wears thick soled shooting boots, and a gray cloak, smokes Indian cigars, uses a cigar holder, and carries a blunt pen-knife in his pocket." Who didn't see *that* coming?

Sherlock's footprint game is *extraordinary.* He's derived evidence from footprints on thousands of different surfaces: clay soil, mud, snow, carpet, ashes, and of course blood. He's such an authority on the matter that he's written a monograph called "The Tracing of Footsteps with Some Remarks on the Uses of Plaster of Paris as a Preserver of Impresses." This guy knows his audience.

Now let's just take a moment and think about how many footprints he will have needed to see in order to make those judgments. He's more adept than a Native American Indian tracker, who has only been doing it for their entire lives. Sherlock definitely shows himself to be above the proverbial 10,000-hour rule of expertise on footprints, as he is with everything in his cases.

Expert in handwriting analysis. Back in Doyle's time, handwriting analysis was highly reliable and got much more credit than it does in modern times. To that end, Holmes keeps current on graphology, the study of handwriting. He uses his mastery to make deductions that stagger the mind—

even so far as to correctly identify the gender and overall character of the original writer. In "The Adventure of the Reigate Spire," Holmes not only correctly guesses that a certain letter was written by two men of very different ages but that they were also related.

In "The Adventure of the Norwood Builder," Holmes analyzes an old construction worker's will at the behest of a lawyer accused of murdering him. Noticing that the writing on the will is shaky in certain parts—as if the writer didn't care how it looked—Holmes figures out that it was written on a train, which would account for the awkward scribblings. Rightly believing that no lawyer would ever write such an important document on a train and in such a sloppy manner, he deduces that the construction worker himself wrote the will while riding the railroad.

In the movie *Sherlock Holmes: A Game of Shadows*, Holmes taunts the archvillain Moriarty by reciting what he's determined about him through his handwriting alone: "The upwards strokes on the P, the J, the M indicate a genius-level intellect. The flourishes on the lower zone denote a highly creative yet meticulous nature. But if one observes the overall slant and pressure of the handwriting, there is a suggestion of acute narcissism, a complete lack of empathy, and pronounced inclination toward... moral insanity." Perhaps Moriarty should learn how to type.

Is the key to being Sherlock Holmes as easy as being an expert in every field in and adjacent to criminal justice? If only it were so easy. That's only half the battle. He also possesses an incredible memory.

An encyclopedic, possibly photographic, memory. Sherlock Holmes has an impossibly good long-term recall. Doyle himself called it a "brain attic," where Holmes would consciously store every small detail about things, people, and places.

Holmes's memory was memorably depicted in a sequence from the BBC show *Sherlock*. Holmes and Watson are tailing a taxi cab through the streets of London. The two are at something of a disadvantage because they're on foot. Throughout the sequence, the screen lays out Sherlock's brain work as a map of London with images of street crossings, signs, and lights.

He has an intimate knowledge of the locale's forced turns and stop signals. Knowing how the taxi will be driven throughout the sequence, Holmes figures out the route the taxi will take and takes a shortcut through buildings and stairs (the map shows how the two of them move in relation to the taxi). At the end of the sequence, he and a very winded Watson reach the taxi's destination before the taxi does.

The scene demonstrated Holmes's uncannily accurate memory of every turn on every street in the city, and the BBC series makes his unquestionable knowledge of London's streets a running theme. Sherlock's comprehensive recall and intense knowledge are parts of who he is—so not only is that scene a pretty exciting action chase, but it's an important sequence of character development.

Keen observer and skillful analyzer of people. In addition to polymathic knowledge and a photographic memory, Sherlock also possesses the observational skills of a hawk. This comes in absorbing information from situations and making sense of it all.

The BBC series *Sherlock* also contains a highly memorable depiction of the first time Holmes meets Watson in his laboratory. Watson has just returned from military service and is looking for a roommate. Without so much as an extended glance, Holmes stuns Watson with the question, "Afghanistan or Iraq?" "Afghanistan," Watson replies with hesitation.

Before he even knows Holmes's name, Watson hears him deduce very intimate details of his life. Holmes knows Watson's relationship with his brother is tense and that they've become alienated from each other. He knows Watson resents his brother because he's an alcoholic and he's just walked out on his wife. He also knows Watson's therapist has told him that his leg limp is psychosomatic—"quite correctly, I'm afraid."

Holmes delivers all these pronouncements in the space of about a half-minute. They're brilliantly straightforward, which is part of Sherlock Holmes's unique intellect. Later, Holmes noticed tan lines on Watson's hands but not on his wrists. This tells Holmes that Watson has just been abroad on business rather than vacation. Holmes also lets Watson know that his stance upon entering his lab gave away the fact that he was in the military—which is why his first question was about whether he was in Afghanistan or Iraq.

We're probably lucky that none of the people in our social circles possess these skills. Dates and parties would either go nowhere or end in brawls.

What Sherlock's Genius Means to You

Sherlock Holmes's genius is impossible to emulate for 99.9% of the world. His incredible skills all come from extensive study and experience. Sure, he may have an IQ of 190. There's probably no chance you can imitate that. But his specialized knowledge comes from study habits that only good discipline can provide—and that discipline *is* something you can emulate.

Holmes's talents are very reliant on objectivity. Even when he's diagnosing a mental or emotional condition, he only uses unbiased data and historical knowledge to make his declarations—the angles of footprints, the layout of London streets, the recurrence of certain characters in a code. Holmes gravitates toward facts and facts alone, supported by reasonable expectations based on his vast memory and knowledge of human behaviors. That objective way of looking at a problem is another thing all of us can copy and practice.

So as unreachable Holmes's talents may seem to the less intellectually elevated, there are facets of what he does so well that anyone can put into practice and develop.

The ability to be observant. Objectively looking at a situation is the key to at least half of the issues we face. This includes watching and perceiving something unfold, "reverse-engineering" or reasoning backward, and coming up with scenarios and answers for every detail, significant or small. (This undoubtedly is how Doyle wrote his Holmes stories—by conjuring up persons in certain situations and back-explaining how they got there.)

It also means being systematic and patient in the way we think instead of rashly jumping to conclusions based on very little information and personal bias. It means absorbing and processing data with great thought and clarity. We just don't really pay attention to our surroundings or look at small details. We're distracted and all over the place. We can improve on this one easily by slowing down and thinking about things more.

Holmes's viewing Watson at their first meeting in the lab and figuring him out shows his powers of observation at work—very, very speedy work. But that kind of observation is easy to use in real life:

- a parent watching their children play with others to see who they get along with

- a chef watching chicken in an oven to determine whether it's close to being done

- a baseball coach observing a batter's swing to see if any mechanics are off

- someone watching the facial tics and behaviors of the other person on a first date

Mastering many domains. Sherlock Holmes's expertise is almost inexhaustible. He's deeply informed on about a million different topics. He has inside knowledge on anything and everything. If he doesn't know something, he knows where to find information quickly. He observes things closely and knows exactly what to look for. And most impressively or insultingly, depending on how you feel, he makes it all look as easy as flipping a light switch.

Holmes is a certified polymath (a person who possesses an expansive knowledge about multiple subjects), and a casual glance through his stories reveals how much he knows: the twists and turns of all the streets in London, what certain handwriting styles indicate, and what every footprint ever left on earth says about the person who left it.

In all honesty, you will never turn into a certified polymath. If it makes you feel better, neither will I. But there's something practical you can learn from Holmes's mastery of several domains: how to *think* like a polymath and develop deep, intellectual curiosity. You can seek to expand the range of your knowledge.

Intellectually curious people go far beyond the surface level of what they see and hear. They don't stop asking "why?" They don't stop asking when they feel comfortable with the answers—they keep plunging into the question at hand until they've peeled away the layers of the situation like an onion.

Some techniques offered by various experts show how to develop and maintain real intellectual curiosity:

- Spending 10 minutes a day learning about something you're interested in but don't know anything about—

French cooking, bacterial strains, the history of the Fender guitar, what people in the Himalayas do for religious rituals (your interest here).

- Learning about subjects directly or peripherally related to a practical aspect of your life. If you're a plumber, you might find yourself more apt to understand how farm irrigation systems work. If you're a barista, maybe you'd find it easier to learn how to home-brew certain drinks.

Thinking outside the box. The term didn't exist until the 1970s, but "thinking outside the box" captures Sherlock Holmes's methodology perfectly. It means considering every angle, choice, and option in a situation. It means using critical thinking to assess what we see and observe. It means applying equational thinking ($x + y = z$) to circumstances in which mathematics wouldn't apparently play a part. It also means flipping the entire equation around and discovering that x, y, and z aren't what you thought they were. And most of all, it means maintaining a relentlessly open mind to all possible interpretations.

Thinking outside the box engages the strongest impulses of our critical minds. It helps us specify what's probable and what isn't. Looking at a problem through unfamiliar viewpoints helps to refocus and reframe it until we arrive at a conclusion that makes perfect, rational sense.

Holmes wasn't one to rule out the unlikely when trying to determine the reality of a situation—in fact, in *The Sign of the Four*, he relished the notion out loud: "How often have I said to you that when you have eliminated the impossible, whatever remains, *however improbable*, must be the truth? We know that he did not come through the door, the window, or the chimney. We also know that he could not have been concealed in the room, as there is no concealment possible. When, then, did he come?"

Holmes thought outside the box when he tried to figure out what was so odd about the construction worker's will. He had no direct evidence about it except the will itself, written with an obviously shaky hand. Nobody would have expected, Holmes included, that someone would write such an important document on a train. But by projecting that as a real possibility—i.e., thinking outside the box—Holmes developed a theory that turned out to be 100% correct.

We have opportunities to think outside the box every day, but because of our dependence on routines and safety nets, we don't often engage them. But the possibilities are limitless:

- Asking the question "What would Van Gogh do?" when deciding how to organize an office.

- Asking a six-year-old child how they would handle a communication problem you're having with an adult friend.

- Writing a poem to diagnose a workplace conflict.

Let's face facts—this book isn't going to turn you into Sherlock Holmes. I know this because writing it didn't turn *me* into Sherlock Holmes. Sometimes, after a beer or two, I might make a passable Watson. But Sherlock Holmes uses brain tools that everyone can access. And using and practicing with those tools develops our brains and makes complex tasks easier to handle. Holmes is a genius because the problems he has to solve require him to be one.

Unless your daily life involves mysterious murders, disappearances, and fraudulent activity—in which case you might want to consider moving—your problems can probably be solved using the same methods Sherlock Holmes uses.

Takeaways:

- Can you think like Sherlock? Yes and no. Let's take a brief jaunt through Sherlock's bibliography to understand this answer.

- Sherlock is an expert in just about every discipline that is in or adjacent to criminal justice. This includes handwriting analysis (at a time when this was more legitimate and relevant), codebreaking, and much more. Sherlock also boasts a photographic memory and the ability to read people like a master FBI interrogator.

- Of course we can't demonstrate these traits to the same degree as Sherlock Holmes, but we can improve the traits that help us solve problems. We can learn to observe and make deductions, we can increase our knowledge in relevant disciplines, and we can also improve our memories. In general, we can learn to think more creatively to generate solutions, which might not be on Sherlock's level but are helpful anyway.

Chapter 2. Thinking Outside The Box

When you're faced with a problem, how do you go about solving it? Do you just stare at it and wait for the solution to miraculously appear in front of you? If so, how many times has that tactic worked thus far? While some may be lucky enough to have the solution suddenly hit them on the head like the proverbial apple falling on Newton's head inspiring the idea for gravity, most of the times it just doesn't happen like that.

So in order to solve problems, especially new and complex ones, you'll need as many tools as possible in your bag to help turn the key and open your brain up to creative solutions.

This chapter will equip you with exactly those tools to help you broaden your horizons as a problem-solver and liberate your mind from the common limitations that hinder you from finding the best solution. See, often the failure to come up with a solution to the problem doesn't arise out of lack of knowledge or a deficit in logical thinking skills.

Rather, it is born of a failure to simply look past self-imposed walls or even recognize that there are walls blocking your view to an obvious solution. In other words, you may be failing to come up with a solution because you've unconsciously limited yourself to looking for answers only within a very narrow box. As an effective remedy to that conundrum, the following tools will hone your ability to solve problems by thinking out of that box. Rules aren't always real, and assumptions aren't always correct. Read on to learn how to avoid these pitfalls.

SCAMPER Method

One of the easiest ways to cultivate out-of-the-box thinking is the SCAMPER method. Pioneered by Bob Eberle to spark creativity during brainstorming sessions, the SCAMPER method stands for seven techniques that help direct thinking toward innovative ideas and solutions: (S) substitute, (C) combine, (A) adapt, (M) minimize/magnify, (P) put to another use, (E) eliminate, and (R) reverse. Collectively, these techniques are based on the idea that you can come up with something new by simply modifying the old things already present around you.

The SCAMPER method works by forcing your mind to think in a new, specific flow, making it possible for you to reach novel solutions. Think of it as akin to opening a faucet that introduces water to seven pipes, and each of those pipes channels to a unique pot of earth. Each pot has the potential to bring forth a new growth once the seeds in it are watered. The SCAMPER method works in a similar way to nurture a new idea or solution out of you.

Note that the SCAMPER method doesn't require that you move in a sequential flow of steps. You may start with any of the thinking techniques it involves and jump among the different techniques throughout your brainstorming or problem-solving session. Furthermore, it adapts the principle of *force-fitting*. This means that in order to come up with fresh solutions, you should be willing to integrate ideas, objects, or elements together—no matter how dissimilar, unrelated, or apparently illogical they seem to be.

Only by freeing your mind enough to connect things you never thought of connecting before can you fully harness each of the following thinking techniques of the SCAMPER method. Indeed, this is a major element of SCAMPER because we are too often held back by our preconceptions and assumptions of what cannot be.

Substitute. This technique refers to replacing certain parts in the product, process, or service with another to solve a problem. To carry out this technique, first consider the situation or problem in light of having many elements—multiple materials, several steps in the process, different times or places at which the process can occur, various markets for the product or service, and the like. Then consider that each and every one of these elements may be replaced with an alternative.

Some questions that might help you get into this flow of thinking include the following: "Could a more cost-effective material replace the current one we're using without sacrificing product quality?" "What part of the process can be switched into a simpler alternative?" "In what other places can we offer our services?"

Let's say you're into the production of craft pieces that use a particular kind of glue as adhesive. However, you find that the glue you use easily dries out and clumps up even when stored properly, leading to wastage and more production costs. To solve this problem, consider brainstorming whether you might use a different adhesive to replace what you're currently using. Another example might be substituting local materials for imported ones, not only reducing costs on your end but also helping the local community in the process.

Combine. This technique suggests considering whether two products, ideas, or steps of a procedure may be combined to produce a single output or process that's better in some way. Two existing products could create something new if put together. Two old ideas could merge into a fresh, groundbreaking one if fused in the right way. Two stages of a process may be melded into one to create a more streamlined, efficient procedure.

Questions that can facilitate a line of thinking utilizing the combined technique include the following: "Can we put two or more elements together?" "Can we carry out two processes at the same time?" "Can we join forces with another company to improve our market strength?"

For instance, the combination of the spoon and fork has led to the innovation of the spork, a utensil now often packed within ready-to-eat noodle cups because of its cost-saving and convenient design. It solves the problem of having to manufacture two different utensils and effectively halves the cost of production.

Adapt. This technique intends to adjust something in order to enhance it. It solves problems by improving on how things are typically done, with adjustments ranging from something small to something radical. It challenges you to think of ways that you can adjust what's already existing—be it a product, a process, or a manner of doing things—such that it solves a current problem and is better tailored to your needs.

Noticing that you have less energy than usual, for instance, you may think of solving the problem by making adjustments to your food choices, such as cutting back on empty calories and processed food. In the business world, this technique is also often utilized by brainstorming groups looking to enhance their product, service, or production process.

Some questions considered under this rubric include the following: "How can we regulate the existing process to save us more time?" "How can we tweak the existing product to sell better?" "How can we adjust the existing process to be more cost-effective?"

An example of an adaptation for a product is the development of mobile phone cases that have been imbued with shock absorbers or shockproof material. This clever tweak has obviously been developed in response to the common problem of accidentally dropping and consequently damaging fragile phone parts. In a similar vein, waterproofing mobile phone cases, wristwatches, and the like is another instance of adapting a product in order to improve it.

Magnify or minimize. This technique involves either increasing or decreasing an element to trigger new ideas and solutions. Magnifying pertains to increasing something, such as by exaggerating a problem, putting more emphasis on an idea, making a product bigger or stronger, or doing a process more frequently.

On the other hand, minimizing entails decreasing something, such as by toning down a problem, deemphasizing an idea, reducing the size of a product, or carrying out a process less frequently. Thinking through certain elements in terms of either magnifying or minimizing them is bound to give you fresh insights as to the most and least significant parts of your problem, thus guiding you toward effective solutions.

Discussion questions that apply the magnify technique include the following: "How can you exaggerate or overstate the problem?" "What would be the outcome if you emphasized this feature?" "Will doing the process more frequently make a difference?" As for minimizing, challenge yourself to ponder on the following: "How will playing down this feature change the outcome?" "How can we condense this product?" "Will doing this step less frequently lead to better efficiency?"

Say that you've been assigned to transfer to a smaller office. You now have the problem of fitting your things into a more confined space. Using the magnify and minimize technique to resolve your dilemma, you can ask yourself questions as to which office components you would want to place more or less emphasis on. Are you going to place more emphasis on having space for receiving and meeting with clients or for tech equipment or maybe for file storage?

Mulling over which aspect to magnify will help you pick out and arrange things in your new office in a way that best reflects your needs and values. As for using the minimize technique, consider which of your office stuff may be condensed together to fit a smaller floor area. For example, while previously you may have had separate tables for your computer and your printer, you may think of using a compact computer desk with a printer shelf instead.

Put to another use. This technique aims to figure out how an existing product or process may be used for a purpose other than what it's currently being used for. It stimulates a discussion on the myriad of other ways you might find a use for anything from raw materials to finished products to discarded waste. It's basically about finding a new purpose for old things.

Some questions that can facilitate this line of thinking include the following: "How else can this product be used?" "Can another part of the company use this material?" "Can we find a use for the bits we throw out?"

Consider how this would apply for stuff lying around in your own home. For instance, how would you address the problem of old newspapers just piling up in a corner? Using them to clean your window panes is a common solution, but how about finding other fresh ways to use them? By challenging yourself to think of more unconventional uses, you will magnify the way those old newspapers benefit you, from serving as trusty deodorizers for shoes to being raw materials for fun papier-mâché crafts.

Eliminate. This technique refers to identifying the unnecessary elements of a project or process so that they can be eliminated and thus provide for an improved outcome. It considers how a procedure may be streamlined by dropping redundant steps or how the same output may be produced despite cutting resources. Whatever resource is freed up may then be used to enhance creativity and innovation.

Questions that make up this rubric include the following: "Is there any step we can remove without affecting the outcome?" "How would we carry out the same activity if we had half the resources?" "What would happen if we eliminated this part?"

One of the most useful applications of this technique is in the area of addressing financial problems in daily life. For example, you find that you're earning enough for your daily expenses but never get to put money aside for emergencies. Barring the option of gaining more income, the only thing left to do is to subtract expenses so you can save for an emergency fund.

Using the eliminate technique, identify expenses you can cut—maybe pass up on buying that shiny new bag you don't really need or opt for cheaper home-cooked meals instead of dining out. The money freed up from eliminating unnecessary expenses can then be your savings for use come rainy days.

Reverse. This technique suggests switching up the order of the process steps in order to find solutions and maximize innovative potentials. Also known as the rearrange technique, this line of thinking encourages interchanging elements or considering the process backward in order to stimulate a fresh take on the situation.

Some questions that apply the reverse technique include the following: "How would reversing the process change the outcome?" "What would happen if we did the procedure backward?" "Can we interchange one step with another?"

Say you're having trouble fulfilling your personal promise to exercise more. You've had it written in your schedule to spend 30 minutes exercising at the end of the day. But when it comes time for it, you always seem to have other more urgent things to attend to or are too tired for it. Thus, you never get around to doing it consistently. To solve this problem, you may consider applying the reverse technique.

Check whether you may interchange your exercise time slot with another part of your day, such as making time for it first thing in the morning instead. By reversing the time you set for exercising, you may just find it easier to stick to the routine, as in the morning you're not yet drained or too beset by the day's activities.

The SCAMPER method is one of the easiest yet most effective strategies for finding solutions to problems and sparking creative thinking. Because a process is explored from seven different perspectives—substitute, combine, adapt, modify, put to another use, eliminate, and reverse—no stone is left unturned, and even unconventional solutions can be uncovered.

By forcing you to think in a specific, unique way, the SCAMPER method jolts your mind out of the regular pattern it's used to running and onto new roads worth exploring. And for every new path you explore, you generate new and varied ideas, creating a pool from which you can later draw the best idea to solve the problem at hand. Where you had one or two ways of looking at a problem, you now have seven additional approaches to apply.

Osborn-Parnes Model

Anyone who's ever attempted to solve a problem knows that it isn't done in an instant. It involves a series of steps that typically work to stretch the mind to broaden perspectives, then narrow it down to specific features, then possibly back to widening the view on the situation, and so on.

In other words, problem-solving involves a repeating cycle of diverge-converge-diverge-converge. This recurring pattern of thought is best incorporated in a problem-solving strategy known as the creative problem-solving (CPS) model.

The CPS model, also known as the Osborn-Parnes model, emerges out of the work of brainstorming and creativity pioneers Alex Osborn and Sidney Parnes. Osborn originated the concept of brainstorming and established the Creative Education Foundation (CEF) in New York, while Parnes headed the CEF for many years and ultimately formalized the CPS model based on Osborn's work. The CPS model outlines six stages of problem-solving: (1) mess-finding, (2) fact-finding, (3) problem-finding, (4) idea-finding, (5) solution-finding, and (6) action-finding or acceptance-finding.

The first three steps are what we typically skip because we are already staring a problem in the face—they are focused on finding shortcomings that can become urgent problems in the future. Thus, the first three steps are more useful if you want to proactively improve or refine something that is still functional or working but you're not sure how to go about it. Most problem-solving methods like SCAMPER are just about generating ideas to deal with a known problem, but they can certainly be used together.

Mess-finding. The first step in the CPS model is all about finding an area of concern. What is the mess of issues, problems, and challenges that warrants a closer look? There are generally two ways you can look at a mess—either you see it as a cringe-worthy muddle and turn away from it or you see it as a plethora of opportunities for uncovering interesting problems.

The CPS model suggests looking for a mess with the latter perspective in mind. Mess-finding is all about spotting a situation that demands attention, one that's necessary or interesting enough to merit your continued engagement as you proceed with the problem-solving process.

For instance, look around your community. What are the messes of interrelated challenges and problems worth looking into more deeply? From a number of apparent community issues, including such areas as safety and security, delivery of health services, sports and recreational programs, and education, you may consider focusing on one "mess" to work out—say, solid waste management.

Fact-finding. Once you've found a mess (i.e., an area of focus), the second step calls for you to fully expand your understanding of that mess. Fact-finding is about engaging with the mess and tinkering with and delving deeper into the bits of it that would be interesting or necessary to consider for problem-solving.

Also known as data-finding, this step thus needs you to do research, explore both the knowns and unknowns of the situation, search for needed or missing information, and basically find out everything you can about the challenge at hand. Collect data with regard to everything from information and facts to opinions and feelings about the matter. This step is all about building a good database for your problem-solving enterprise.

If you've selected solid waste management as the mess you're going to focus on, fact-finding will involve investigating the current policies and practices of your community with regard to it. Find out how rubbish from each household and establishment is collected, transported, disposed of, and recycled. Gather historical data on any major health and environmental problems that your community might have faced because of improper waste disposal. You may also look into other communities' policies to benchmark for best practices on solid waste management. Leave no stone unturned, because any judgment made with incomplete information is destined to be flawed (even if it is correct).

Problem-finding. Once you've established a substantial knowledge pool, it's time to do some zeroing in on the heart of the situation. In this third step, known as problem-finding, you are invited to use everything you know about the matter to come up with a specific problem statement that expresses just what exactly is problematic in the situation. In other words, which specific knot in a jungle of intertwined issues and challenges are you aiming to untangle? This step helps converge your thinking on a problem that's specific enough so that you can concentrate your mental energy toward productive and feasible ends.

When it comes to solid waste management, for instance, you'll need to examine the data you've collected during fact-finding to look for more specific problems you can feasibly find a solution for. Narrow down your focus on a particularly bothersome or urgent problem within the mess you've chosen— for example, focus on the problem of managing plastic waste.

Idea-finding. After discovering a suitable problem, your next task is to come up with as many ideas as possible to solve that problem. This fourth step is called idea-finding, also known as brainstorming. This is where we typically start with most problems because we already know what we want to overcome or solve, and this is what we need the most help with.

In the previous step, problem-finding, you needed to engage in convergent thinking— that is, narrowing down a number of possible ideas to find the best one, that single problem you want to focus on. In this current step of idea-finding, you'll be called to do the reverse: divergent thinking.

Divergent thinking is a thought process whereby you attempt to generate as many spontaneous ideas as possible, with little concern as to whether they're logical, correct, or valid. While convergent thinking is linear and restricts your thought to finding a single correct or best answer, divergent thinking is nonlinear and expands your mind to explore as many creative answers as you can.

Idea-finding calls for divergent thinking, needing you to stretch your mind in new and different ways to tackle the problem at hand. The more numerous, novel, and diverse the ideas and solutions you come up with, the better! In this step, you are not to evaluate any of those ideas yet; you simply need to generate as many of them as possible. Don't hesitate to jot down a possible solution for fear that it's too far-fetched, illogical, or idealistic.

Evaluating only puts a stopper to creativity, and you don't need to do it at this point. Simply let the ideas flow and note every single one of them. In fact, this is where you can use SCAMPER in conjunction with the CPS method.

For instance, brainstorm ideas on how your community could manage plastic wastes. Posing this question to a group of community members, you may generate such ideas as implementing segregation schemes, reusing, recycling, urging people to bring their own shopping bags, holding info campaigns on proper plastic disposal, and so on. Even if you think you've brainstormed a winner, keep generating ideas and don't stop or limit yourself.

Solution-finding. Now that you have generated a diverse collection of ideas, possible solutions, and alternatives, the next step is to converge on a solution that would offer you the most effective way of tackling the identified problem. This is where evaluation comes in. It's time to consider each of the ideas you've noted from the previous step in light of objective criteria, assessing for such factors as suitability, usefulness, feasibility, cost-effectiveness, and the like.

The solution-finding step is all about looking at the relative strengths and weaknesses of all the possible solutions you had generated in order to hash out the best one, the one solution that offers the highest chance for problem resolution and the fewest barriers for implementation.

For example, after generating a list of ideas for managing plastic wastes, evaluate each idea for viability with respect to such factors as costs, time requirement, required manpower, available equipment, local government support, and acceptance of the community members to implement such ideas. Consider the pros and cons of each suggested action or policy, and decide on which ones would be feasible and most effective for your community.

Action-finding. Finally, once you've determined the best solution you want to apply to your problem, the final step in the process is to formulate a plan of action. Also called acceptance-finding, this step is all about outlining your needs, any foreseeable obstacles, long-term milestones, and specific short-term actions for resolving the problem. Carefully draft a good plan that implements your chosen solution, and once you're satisfied with that plan, accept that course of action and carry it out.

So with regard to the problem of your community's plastic refuse, for instance, this final step would see you create a plastic waste management plan. This plan may combine several useful ideas you'd identified in the solution-finding step of the process. Outline a plan of action from plastic use reduction to plastic waste collection, disposal, and recycling.

The six stages of the CPS model—mess-finding, fact-finding, problem-finding, idea-finding, solution-finding, and action-finding—are a carefully outlined sequence to guide you toward the best solution. More than just a technique that limits you to a linear problem-solving process, though, this model incorporates steps that require divergent thought. In so doing, the CPS model ensures that you expand your mind to explore unconventional ideas, helping you think outside the box on your way to finding the solution.

Intentional Constraints

When it comes to creativity, it's common for people to equate it with the idea of abundance—an abundance of materials, time, and other resources is easily seen as effective prompters of fresh ideas and innovative solutions. An artist given a wealth of art supplies and provisions is seen as being in wonderland, with the highest chances of turning out with a uniquely crafted masterpiece.

A chef provided with a huge variety of the best ingredients is easily imagined as having everything needed to churn out an inspired dish. The prevalent idea is that the more that is loaded into the creative's arsenal, the better the output will be. The more ideas and freedom, the better a chance you will have to generate a solution to your problems.

But is that the best method to solve problems or the best way to spur the flow of fresh ideas and solutions? There is a big difference between the two.

Compared to piling on the resources and broadening options, putting up constraints and limiting resources appear to spark creativity better. Psychologist and creativity expert Patricia Stokes of Columbia University has seen such a principle at work in an experiment she conducted in 1993. Her study demonstrated how rodents constrained to press a bar using only their right paws resulted in those rodents devising more creative ways of pressing the bar, compared to rodents that were free to use all their limbs.

This is what's known as "little 'c' creativity," a form of creativity aimed at addressing practical problems rather than yielding artistic output. And with the number and complexity of emerging 21st-century problems needing resourceful solutions in the face of scarcity, "little 'c' creativity" may be the next big thing.

To test how people's creative use of resources may be influenced by thinking about scarcity or abundance, Ravi Mehta and Meng Zhu conducted a study using "the bubble wrap test" in 2015. They predicted that thinking about scarcity would boost people's capacity to use resources in unconventional ways.

To test that prediction, Mehta and Zhu randomly divided 60 undergrads into two groups. One group was instructed to write an essay about growing up with scarce resources, while the other group was to write about growing up with abundant resources. Both groups were then tasked to come up with a solution for a real problem their university faced: how to put to good use 250 bubble wrap sheets that were byproducts of a recent move of their computer lab.

After drafting a proposal for using the bubble wrap, the participants answered a survey on the different ways they tackled the problem.

Twenty judges, blind to the participants' scarcity or abundance groupings, then scored the proposals in terms of the novelty of the ideas they put forward. The result? The scarcity group outperformed the abundance group in coming up with creative uses for the discarded bubble wrap.

The outcome of Mehta and Zhu's experiment reveals a counterintuitive but valuable point in the science of creativity— that sometimes, in order to force the mind to think out of the box, it is necessary to first make that box smaller and smaller, reining in the mind with fewer and fewer options so it has no choice but to reconstruct those options in unconventional ways. In other words, creativity appears to be less of an inborn personality trait and more of a response to environments and situations that compel the person to make the best use of whatever resource is available.

Say you're part of a marketing team tasked to come up with a print ad promoting your new product. If you were told you can fill an entire magazine with promotional information about your product, chances are you'll end up with something that may be highly informative and detailed but overloaded with irrelevant details that will only bore prospective consumers instead of enticing them to buy your merchandise.

But if you deliberately constrain your ad to, say, a quarter of a page, your team is likely to generate vastly more interesting and eye-catching ad ideas. Precisely because you are given so little space to work with, you'll be forced to come up with the catchiest of taglines and the most striking of images to get your product noticed.

The following are more examples of how creative constraints can give rise to impressive solutions to the problems in front of you.

Six-word memoirs. Can an entire life be summed up in just six words? The book *Not*

Quite What I Was Planning proves that the answer is yes—and with results ranging from the amusing to the profound, too. While traditional memoirs are often thick volumes filled with elaborate details and analysis of a life's beginnings, highlights, and struggles, *Not Quite What I Was Planning* breaks such a mold by showcasing a collection of six-word memoirs. Interesting examples include Stephen Colbert's "Well, I thought it was funny" and Linda Williamson's "Painful nerd kid, happy nerd adult." How about you? How would you sum up your life in six words?

As this creative venture shows, setting constraints on your projected output can lead to interesting results. Putting parameters on what you're allowed to produce—in this case, no more than six words to encapsulate an entire life—forces your brain to be more imaginative so as to meet the parameters without sacrificing the output's meaningfulness. Without such constraints on expected output, you'll be more likely to stick to just comfortable yet uninteresting solutions.

But introduce constraints and you're on your way toward generating creative ideas you didn't imagine you had in you to produce.

Career-ending injury. They say every dark cloud has a silver lining. Artist Phil Hansen has proven that right, though he had to do more than just spot the silver lining. He had to suffer the dark cloud for years, then decide to create its silver lining. Phil had developed a specific pointillist style all throughout his years as an art student but unfortunately met an injury that rendered him incapable of practicing the same technique ever again. Distraught and hopeless, he left the art world.

But though Phil tried to leave the artist in him behind, he later found that nothing could take the artist out of him. Three years later, he started to dabble in the arts again. But constrained by the repercussions of his injury, he had to develop a new art style that incorporated the shaky lines his quivering hands couldn't help making.

Embracing rather than resenting the constraints that his injury had put on him, Phil was thus led to create unique and amazing art pieces only he could create— not despite his injury, but because of it.

Phil's story illustrates how even limitations in personal capacity can serve as the trigger to produce more creative and unique outcomes. Not being able to do things in the same way you've always done them may be a hard pill to swallow, but in certain situations, that may be the very push you need to be more creative and discover new (often better) ways of doing things.

If you find yourself constrained by your own incapacity to do things a certain way, take it as a challenge to change the way things have always been done. With this perspective, you'll be able to come up with ideas that may not just get things done but revolutionize how they're done.

Physical limitations. Trying to solve real-world problems almost always involves physical limitations. The materials could be finite, the physical space for the project may be limited, and the world naturally follows laws of physics that everyone must contend with. These constraints affect many problem situations needing practical solutions, as well as creative endeavors that require perceptiveness for them to work out magnificently.

One of the artists who has shown that embracing the constraints of physical limitations may well lead to unique art projects is Michael Johansson. To push his creative instincts to the edge, Michael chooses frames to work within. He challenges himself to create art pieces that fit together used objects within each frame, much like a real-life Tetris challenge.

These frames vary in size from luggage-sized ones to entire walls, and the intricacy in his task lies in filling up these frames in such a way that the objects within them—which range from books to whole cars—fit together neatly like pieces of a puzzle. Each frame is a physical constraint that stretches his mind to think of ways random objects can be puzzled together within it, giving birth to interesting art pieces that guarantee a second look from everyone who comes across them.

Michael's creative projects are proof of how constraints in the physical aspects of an undertaking can compel the mind to think more creatively. When the space within which you can work is limited, you'll be forced to find ways the elements you need can fit together like puzzle pieces forming a cohesive picture.

You can see this principle at work when you discover how creative you can get while packing your suitcase, just so everything you need to put in there fits. All of a sudden, you have new ways of folding clothes, incorporating certain items within others, and arranging things so every bit of space is maximized. The same thing happens when you try to work through a problem with set confines—you get more creative at finding ways to make sure everything "fits."

Copyright restrictions. Poets are artists of their own kind, wordsmiths that gather their material from the seemingly endless constellation of words available to them at any given time. But what if even words are given to a poet in a limited fashion? Will that limit the poet's creativity or enhance it?

In the case of artist Austin Kleon, such constraint definitely boosts creativity. Known for his newspaper blackout poems, Austin takes a newspaper page or column and then blacks out words using a marker until only his own poem or message is left visible. In addition to the limited words he has to work with, Austin also has copyright restrictions to consider because he's using printed material written by someone else.

Needing to work in accordance with copyright law, Austin is thus driven to creatively flesh out poems that either reverse, parody, or completely differ from the original message of the newspaper piece. Rather than limiting inspiration or originality, restrictions thus have the effect of spurring on imagination and creativity.

As Austin's inspired works illustrate, restricting the materials available for you to work with can get your creative juices flowing and lead you to produce remarkable output. While Austin's materials were words, yours may be a host of different resources, including money, product supplies, tools, and other provisions. What Austin's process proves is that limiting those resources doesn't necessarily have to equal to a decline in creativity.

On the contrary, by having no choice but to make use only of what's already available in short supply, you're forcing yourself to think out of the box. Precisely because you have such limited resources, it's your imagination that has to fill the gap by stretching itself to discover innovative solutions and ideas.

Work-Rest Balance

The first three strategies of sharpening out-of-the-box thinking discussed above—the

SCAMPER method, the Osborn-Parnes model, and intentional constraints—are all about hustle, hustle, hustle. Indeed, when it comes to thinking creatively in order to solve problems, putting in hard work and persevering at coming up with novel ideas are important.

However, what many people forget is that when it comes to creative problem-solving, the hustle is only half of the equation. The other half—taking time to simply rest and not work—is just as important. Much like how athletes need recovery periods scheduled into their training program to condition them best, you too need recovery periods for you to be optimized for creative work. There are two main ways you can engage in these recovery periods: breaks and naps.

Breaks. Do you always feel guilty about taking a break from racking your brain trying to solve a problem? Psychologists and cognitive experts say you shouldn't. It turns out breaks are integral to engaging a mode in your brain that facilitates creative thinking.

According to Barbara Oakley, engineering professor and author of *A Mind for Numbers: How to Excel at Math and Science (Even If You Flunked Algebra)*, the brain has two modes: focused and diffused. When you're attempting to learn something new or actively working on cognitively demanding tasks, you run on focused mode.

In this mode, what's hard at work is mainly your brain's prefrontal cortex, the region responsible for higher-order thinking skills such as planning, evaluation, and decision-making. To concentrate your attention and thinking, your brain blocks your access to the other mode—the diffuse mode—every time you're focusing.

However, Professor Oakley points out that there are important learning and processing mechanisms that occur in the diffuse mode of your cognitive life. The diffuse mode runs whenever you're relaxed, such as when you're taking a leisurely walk or drifting into a daydream. In this mode, multiple brain areas other than your prefrontal cortex are activated.

In the diffuse mode, your mind is actually more adept at spotting patterns where it has previously seen none, putting together seemingly disparate elements in ingenious ways and coming up with novel and inspired solutions to very complex problems.

As psychologist Scott Barry Kaufman argues, it is through such diffuse mind wandering that you get to carry out such adaptive functions as running through different information streams, disentangling multiple concerns, and triggering creative ideas. So while you may think you're simply taking a leisurely walk during that break from brainstorming, your brain is actually running processes that'll ultimately take you from stumped to enlightened as you attempt to crack that problem.

Okay, so it's good to take a break—that much is clear. But the next question now becomes, when should you take these breaks? Do you take a break every time you feel like it, or should you schedule your breaks at regular intervals?

Researchers say that for optimum creativity, the latter would be the better option. Scheduling regular breaks from tackling a particular problem, be it by switching to a different problem or stepping away from any problem-solving activity altogether, has been shown to improve people's capacity to come up with effective and novel solutions.

Evidence for the effectiveness of such approach has been demonstrated by studies conducted by Jackson Lu, Modupe Akinola, and Malia Mason. In their experiments, participants were randomly assigned to one of three approaches: (1) spending the first half of the time trying to solve one problem and the second half trying to solve a second problem, (2) regularly switching between the two problems at predetermined intervals, and (3) switching between the problems at the participants' own discretion.

While many might instinctively prefer the third approach, thinking the autonomy and flexibility it allows boosts creativity and prevents being unnecessarily stuck, the results told a different story. It was those who switched between the problems at predetermined intervals that showed significantly higher chances of finding the right answer or generating the most novel ideas for both problems.

How does scheduling regular breaks produce better outcomes than the other approaches? The researchers say that such breaks refresh your perspective and approach to the problem or task at hand. And because the breaks are scheduled, you don't run the risk of keeping at a single task, seemingly persevering forward but actually going in circles as you come up with more and more redundant ideas as time passes by. Taking regular, scheduled breaks keeps your ideas fresh and diverse, giving you the highest chances of arriving at the best solutions and creative outcomes.

Naps. Feel like taking a nap in the midst of tackling a difficult problem? Go ahead, researchers say. Cognitive scientists and creativity experts agree that napping helps you perform better at problem-solving by giving you the following three cognitive benefits.

First, the stage of sleep known as REM (rapid eye movement), when most dreaming occurs, has been shown by numerous studies to be vital to creativity. One such study, conducted by Harvard Medical School, tested participants in a number of creativity tasks after being woken in different stages of sleep. Results revealed that those woken during REM sleep while they were dreaming performed 32% better in the creativity tests, compared to those woken during deep sleep when the brain was resting with no dreams taking place. This finding led the researchers to propose that REM sleep stimulates the brain to fresh ways of thinking and makes it more flexible for unconventional yet inspired thoughts to come through.

Second, napping is known to recharge your brain and invigorate your body, helping you be better primed for finding creative solutions to complex problems. Napping helps facilitate cell repair, maintain heart health, and keep your hormones well-regulated, not to mention assists in giving you a more youthful look, a fitter and more active body, and a longer life.

Cognitively, the way napping recharges your brain rouses your alertness and improves your creative insight. And when you have a well-rested body prepped for action and a rejuvenated mind primed for perceptiveness, what problem could be too hard to solve?

Finally, napping has been shown to improve memory retention. Problem-solving and creativity both rely at least partly on your ability to retain details about situations and events long enough for you to see patterns and connections that will eventually help you arrive at the best solution. Napping can help you in that regard—improving your memory retention so the facts and information you've observed are retained for good use later.

Evidence for the positive effects of napping on memory retention has been demonstrated by several studies. In one such study by Walker, 39 healthy young adults were each assigned to either the nap group or the no-nap group. At 12 noon, both groups were given a memory task that required them to retain a lot of information. At 2:00 p.m., the nap group went to sleep for an hour and a half, while the no-nap group stayed awake. Then, at 6:00 p.m., both groups were given a new set of learning challenges.

Who performed better at the 6:00 p.m. tasks? If you guessed the nap group, you're right. Walker suggested that napping must've acted as an important clearing or prepping mechanism for the brain's short-term memory storage, resulting in the nap group having an enhanced capacity for retaining new information.

Thus, though to some people taking breaks and napping may seem like slacking off, to the informed they are essential activities that contribute to the success of the problem-solving and creative processes. Refusing to take breaks or depriving yourself of invigorating naps is likely to result only in burnout, not to mention failure to find solutions to tricky problems. For the best ideas and most creative solutions, make sure to balance working with periods of rest.

Altered States of Consciousness

To come up with creative solutions to problems, often the problem-solving process itself needs to be creative. Traditional, logical, and conscious methods of solving a problem, such as via the famous scientific method, are not always effective at driving you to come up with ingenious ways of solving complex problems.

Sometimes, you'll need to carry out unique strategies of stimulating and coaxing your mind such that creative new insights bubble up to the surface. These unique strategies may not always be of the scientific, conscious kind. Rather, they are likely to be born of an artistic bent, utilizing a level of consciousness that's not completely "there." This section discusses two such unique strategies involving altered states of consciousness—sleepiness and daydreaming.

Sleepiness. While being sleepy can easily be thought of as a state where creative problem-solving capacity becomes impaired, researchers are shining light on evidence that says otherwise. It turns out that sleepiness, and in the same vein drunkenness, can actually work wonders for improving your ability to solve problems that require creative insight.

This is mainly because, in such states as sleepiness and drunkenness, your brain loses its normal focus on details it considers relevant. And while for tackling standard analytic problems such loss of focus may constitute a drawback, for dealing with creative problem-solving, that loss of focus is precisely what you need. This certainly makes the proclivity of some of our most famous artists and their compulsions for substance abuse more logical.

In support of the above notion, author Jonah Lehrer highlights several studies that illustrated how the grogginess of a sleepy or drunk brain can actually improve creative problem-solving ability. In one study, a group of patients with brain injury resulting in severe attention deficits performed significantly better at solving creatively challenging puzzles compared to normal participants. Likewise, another study showed that groggy students did better at solving creative problems, and still another study showed similar results after challenging drunk students to tackle such tests. The lack of focus brought on by cognitive deficit, sleepiness, or drunkenness appeared to have allowed the participants a more diffuse way of thinking, such that they got to consider a wider range of possibilities as their imaginations ran free.

But what exactly is at work in those groggy or sleepy brains that helps rouse creative powers of greater proportions? Neuroscientists have joined in the search for an answer as well, and they're shining the spotlight on what's known as *theta waves.*

Theta waves are a kind of brain wave present during periods when you're halfway between sleep and wakefulness or between deep daydreaming and active alertness. During such "theta states," you're not fully awake but not quite asleep either. Such states also include times when you're engaged in such a monotonous or automatic task (e.g., freeway driving, brushing your hair) that you mentally disengage from it and wander into a state that's deeply relaxed but short of sleeping.

According to educator Ned Herrmann, it's during the theta state that people often get good ideas and creative insights, because in such a state, thought censorship is suspended, thoughts move more freely, and creative juices flow more abundantly.

Salvador Dali, renowned surrealist and dubbed painter of dreams, is known for utilizing the technique he called "slumber with a key" to get himself in such a halfway dream state, also known as hypnagogic sleep. In this technique, Dali sits in his chair holding a key, which is poised just above an upside-down plate. As he dozes off, his hand drops the key, which loudly clangs onto the plate and jolts him to wakefulness.

Dali said this immerses him to the briefest of naps, not longer than a quarter of a second, and the feeling of having barely lost consciousness for such a fleeting moment revives his physical and psychic being into an immensely creative state. In this way, he keeps himself on the edge of consciousness and unconsciousness effectively to reap the rewards of theta waves.

If following Dali's key technique seems a little too dramatic for your taste, there are other methods you can do in daily life to take advantage of that theta or halfway dream state toward improving your flair for problem-solving. As writer Kate Rodriguez suggests, practice thinking of the most pressing problem or immediate task you need to accomplish for the day just as you begin to wake in the morning.

Reflect on that concern while your eyes are still closed and your brain still feels a bit dreamy or groggy. During this half-asleep state, let your brain ruminate on a single problem or task, without consciously forcing it to take a specific solution route. Simply allow your mind to sit with that problem. If you happen upon a useful idea or solution in that process, grab a pen and paper or your phone and note down your ideas there so you don't let them slip away into nothingness once you gain full consciousness. Later, revisit these inspired ideas and polish them into a workable solution.

Daydreaming. If you've ever suffered through an extremely boring class, chances are you've drifted off to a daydream, entertaining thoughts completely irrelevant to your immediate surroundings. And if your teacher happened to have caught you daydreaming, chances are she must've told you off for being unfocused and lazy.

Daydreaming has traditionally been regarded by many in a rather negative light, seeing it as a sign of a mind lacking the drive and focus essential for success. But recent studies on cognitive science are revealing an interesting twist on this notion. It turns out that rather than serving as a hindrance to productivity, daydreaming actually boosts creativity and is essential for creative, innovative thinking.

While daydreaming appears to be a mindless activity, neuroscience shows that the term "mindless" is not quite appropriate. During daydreaming, several parts of the brain show increased activity. When you daydream, your brain's "default network" runs and immerses you in a state of wakeful rest, in which you detach focus from your surroundings and let your mind wander more freely. In such a state, your mind becomes more flexible to consider unusual concepts and unconventional ways of thinking.

You thus become better at divergent thinking, a mode essential for creativity as it leads you to come up with a more numerous and diverse set of ideas and potential solutions to ill-defined problems. This is another part of our brains that simply isn't available when we're supposedly fully conscious and present.

Furthermore, neuroscience has demonstrated that, in addition to the activation of the default network, daydreaming also sparks activity in parts of the brain involved in high-level, complex problem-solving. So while you may think daydreaming is an act of moving away from the task of finding solutions or answers, it's actually an effective mechanism for running background processes in your brain that keep working at finding creative ideas and solutions.

These background processes that run even as you're mindlessly engaged in an unrelated activity make up what's known as incubation in the context of problem-solving.

You may have experienced the fruits of the incubation process when, after giving brainstorming a rest for several days, a brilliant idea comes to you as you're taking a shower. These "shower thoughts" and other similar occurrences may appear like heaven-sent inspirations, but they're actually the product of the incubation process that has continued running in your brain even after you'd given up consciously thinking about solutions.

When you daydream and zone out in the shower, these thoughts are now allowed to rise into the forefront of your mind. Much like how the shoemaker's elves keep working throughout the night to help the shoemaker accomplish his task, your brain keeps working through the details of your problem while daydreaming.

Combinatory Play

We've already mentioned the importance of taking breaks and what sleep can do for your mind. But there's a certain way to take breaks called "combinatory play." It's so good that it was even approved by Albert Einstein.

The most notable scientist of the 20th century was known for taking time out of his work to play the violin. Reportedly, he was even very good at it, as he was with the piano. But while sawing away on the violin during his breaks, Einstein actually arrived at some breakthroughs in his research and philosophical questionings. Allegedly one of these musical sessions was the spark for his most famous equation: $E=mc^2$.

Einstein came up with the term "combinatory play" to describe the intangible process in which his favorite pastime led to ideas that revolutionized the whole of scientific thought. He explained his reasoning as best he could in 1945 in a letter to French mathematician Jacques S. Hadamard:

"My Dear Colleague:

In the following, I am trying to answer in brief your questions as well as I am able. I am not satisfied myself with those answers and I am willing to answer more questions if you believe this could be of any advantage for the very interesting and difficult work you have undertaken.

(A) The words or the language, as they are written or spoken, do not seem to play any role in my mechanism of thought. The psychical entities which seem to serve as elements in thought are certain signs and more or less clear images which can be "voluntarily" reproduced and combined.

There is, of course, a certain connection between those elements and relevant logical concepts. It is also clear that the desire to arrive finally at logically connected concepts is the emotional basis of this rather vague play with the above-mentioned elements. But taken from a psychological viewpoint, this combinatory play seems to be the essential feature in productive thought—before there is any connection with logical construction in words or other kinds of signs which can be communicated to others.

(B) The above-mentioned elements are, in my case, of visual and some of muscular type. Conventional words or other signs have to be sought for laboriously only in a secondary stage, when the mentioned associative play is sufficiently established and can be reproduced at will.

(C) According to what has been said, the play with the mentioned elements is aimed to be analogous to certain logical connections one is searching for.

(D) Visual and motor. In a stage when words intervene at all, they are, in my case, purely auditive, but they interfere only in a secondary stage, as already mentioned.

(E) It seems to me that what you call full consciousness is a limit case which can never be fully accomplished. This seems to me connected with the fact called the narrowness of consciousness (Enge des Bewusstseins)."

Einstein seemed to believe that indulging in his creative tendencies was helpful for his logical and rational pursuits. That might have been the case, and it also might have been the case that to engage in a distraction was helpful for taking on different perspectives and viewing things from different angles.

However, combinatory play is different from other creativity techniques in this chapter because it takes the reality that no idea is purely original and created in a vacuum. In other words, there was something related to playing the violin and Einstein's famous theory of relativity. What was this similarity? We don't know, but it's sufficient that it spurred some kind of epiphany from Einstein.

Combinatory play is not simply the notion that play takes your mind to a different world to regroup. It recognizes, as Einstein did, that taking pieces of knowledge and insight from different disciplines and combining them in new contexts is how most creativity truly happens. So as mentioned, somehow Einstein saw something in playing the violin that helped him think about physics in an entirely new way. It is not unlike elements of SCAMPER, and it encourages us to step outside our own box of comfort in seeking creative solutions.

The lesson here is to engage in your own pursuits and not feel constrained by having to stay in similar or adjacent disciplines, thinking that they will aid you. More of the same probably will not help; a dash of something different just might.

To wrap up, creative problem-solving requires the ability to expand your thinking beyond the narrow confines of traditional thought. You'll need to be able to think out of the box, and a number of effective tools are available to help you do just that. Through the SCAMPER method, you may facilitate the birth of innovative ideas by directing your mind to think in seven specific flows: substitute, combine, adapt, modify, put to another use, eliminate, and reverse.

Using the Osborn-Parnes creative problem-solving (CPS) model, you can engage your mind in a cycle of divergent and convergent thinking toward the formulation of a viable solution. You may also choose to impose intentional constraints, deliberately limiting your resources and options to force your mind to be creative enough to come up with unconventional solutions.

Also remember that certain techniques for sharpening out-of-the-box thinking call for you not to be hard at work in straining ideas out of your brain, but instead allowing your mind to rest and drift off to altered states of consciousness. Taking breaks, napping, being in a state halfway between sleep and wakefulness, and allowing yourself to daydream are all ways by which you can nurture conditions in your brain that facilitate creative problem-solving. These all take advantage of lesser-used parts of our brains, such as theta waves, diffuse thinking, and the default network. Through the techniques you learned in this chapter, you're better equipped with a freer mind and broader horizons to formulate novel ideas and imaginative solutions.

Takeaways:

- Thinking outside the box is how you can attack a problem or situation from different angles. Staring at a problem through the same lens will rarely yield results, so it's typically necessary to engage in ways that are entirely foreign to you. You are expanding your set of mental tools in this chapter.
- SCAMPER is a tool for creative thinking, as it provides seven distinct ways of approaching a problem: (S) substitute, (C) combine, (A) adapt, (M) minimize/magnify, (P) put to another use, (E) eliminate, and (R) reverse.
- The Osborn-Parnes model is typically known as the creative problem-solving method. It consists of a few steps as well, though most of us start from step four because this Osborn-Parnes model deals with situations where you're not sure what the problem even is: (1) mess-finding, (2) fact-finding, (3) problem-

finding, (4) idea-finding, (5) solution-finding, and (6) action-finding or acceptance-finding.

- Creating intentional constraints can force creativity because they require innovation to make something work. There are numerous examples provided, such as dealing with copyright violations, but it can be as simple as asking "What if we had to do things in this certain way?"
- Altered states of consciousness have been shown to contribute to creativity. This occurs specifically with regards to sleepiness and daydreaming. When you are sleepy, what are known as theta waves are released in spades, and these aid creativity. Salvador Dali was known to take advantage of this so-called hypnagogic phase of sleep by falling asleep holding a key over a plate, so when he fell asleep, the key would fall and the ensuing noise would wake him up. Daydreaming takes advantage of the fact that when we are in that state, we tend to engage in divergent thinking versus convergent thinking.

- Finally, combinatory play, as popularized by Albert Einstein, is not simply about playing and distracting oneself from the task at hand. Actually, it's about the startling unoriginality of creativity. Everything is derivative, inspired by something else, and otherwise interrelated. Thus, when you engage in combinatory play, you are taking elements from extremely different disciplines and mashing them together subconsciously.

Chapter 3. Observations and Deductive Reasoning

"Once you eliminate the impossible, whatever remains, no matter how improbable, must be the truth." – Sherlock Holmes

How does Sherlock Holmes solve the most mystifying of enigmas? While it's easy to ascribe to him innate super-sleuthing skills bordering on the supernatural, a closer look at the specific techniques he uses reveals that they aren't necessarily powers that defy the laws of the natural world. In fact, his superior mystery-solving ability is simply a product of mastering common skills all of us humans are capable of doing—gathering information and then using that information to arrive at conclusions.

But if that's the case, then why aren't we all going around untangling mysteries and solving conundrums like pros as what Sherlock Holmes does? Well, aside from the fact that we have our own day jobs to tend to, most of us haven't really mastered those basic skills of gathering and using information to the best of our human capacities. We get bombarded by a barrage of information all the time, but we rarely ever get to maximize it to achieve the best results possible.

In other words, we haven't really honed our ability to gather the most information possible in a situation (i.e., our observation skills) and our ability to glean the appropriate conclusions and judgments based on that information (i.e., our deductive reasoning skills). While Sherlock Holmes has perfected the art of gathering and using information to solve mysteries, we have been content to go about life half-blind and oblivious to the ways we can still improve ourselves and our lives just by giving a little more effort into sharpening our skills in observation and deduction.

Take, for instance, Lionel, a marketing assistant about to deliver a big presentation to a hotshot client. Not being much of a techie person, he's nervous about setting up a PowerPoint slideshow in a conference venue that's new to him, but he's relieved to see that the LCD projector in the room is a model he's familiar with. While he's setting up, the client and his posse arrive and settle in. Lionel confidently turns the projector on and adjusts the settings of his laptop to enable the display to be projected on the big screen. Everyone waits for the projector to start showing the slides, but it doesn't.

Lionel fumbles with keys on his laptop, buttons in the projector, and wires in the power source, but to no avail. It goes on for a while, well past the time the presentation should've started by. Lionel begins to panic and sweat through his shirt as the client starts glancing at his watch in impatience. Lionel is sure he's used the same laptop for the same projector before, but why does it seem like the two are incompatible now? Why couldn't he get the thing to work?

Frustrated, he takes a step back and withdraws from all the laptop and projector settings he's been burying his nose in for the last 15 minutes. He surveys the scene and tries to better observe what else he could be missing. Then he sees his glaring mistake—he never connected his laptop to the LCD projector!

How many times have we had such an experience ourselves and have all but banged our heads against the wall for how stupid we were? But the fact is, such mistakes are really not about lacking smarts but about simply lacking the ability to observe well. Lionel tried to solve the problem by diving into such actions as troubleshooting equipment settings and other fancy solutions, but he missed the simplest detail of first seeing to it that the two main pieces of equipment were in fact connected.

The information he needed to solve the problem in one move was right in front of him, but he wasn't able to address it promptly because he failed to properly observe. To help you avoid making such simple yet potentially damaging mistakes, this chapter will be all about techniques to sharpen your observations skills, as well as strategies to hone your ability to make sound deductions based on what you observe.

Observations

Observation is the act of examining something for the purpose of gaining information. You may see and hear a myriad of things at any given point in time, but it doesn't mean you gain information from them—because in actuality, you don't observe them. Observation goes beyond simply seeing and hearing things and instead encompasses absorbing the most information you can from a particular situation. In other words, observation is a process that requires active participation on your part. It's not something you're born with; it's something you develop.

So if you want to master the art of observation, what do you need to do? As in developing any skill, it will require deliberate practice using the right set of techniques. This section offers five effective techniques to bring your observation skill level at par even with Sherlock Holmes: (1) become more detail-oriented, (2) give your 100% focus, (3) note differences from baseline, (4) understand people's self-perceptions, and (5) see the big picture.

Become more detail-oriented. Observation is largely a matter of paying attention to details. This is easier said than done, because again, observation is not simply a matter of sensing things. It requires a deliberate effort to truly see things when you look them and to make mental notes about what you're seeing. It also takes conscious attention to actually listen to what you're hearing and digest those individual sounds apart from other noises in the background.

You may think you're aware of a lot of things all the time, but you'll be surprised to discover how much you've really missed once you start to challenge yourself to observe more intensely and more consistently. While seasoned or highly experienced observers like Sherlock may be able to pick up on a lot of details after simply giving things a casual look (or if you're lucky enough to have expertise in this particular discipline), this is rarely the case for most. To become more detail-oriented, you'll need to put in conscious effort to look, notice, and remember the specifics of what you observe.

For example, what is to the immediate left and right of you right now? Chances are you have no idea. Now take five seconds to look at what's above you, below you, on your right, and on your left. Can you name five things or details you saw in each direction? Chances are, you'll realize again that you may have looked in each direction but failed to see the details that made up each scene.

Say you did this exercise in your office, a familiar setting where you spend hours upon hours. When you looked overhead, you may have seen the ceiling, but did you noticed how many lighting fixtures there were? How are the lighting fixtures shaped? Are the ceiling grids linear or curved? Are the ceiling panels smooth or textured? Are there any loose or damaged ceiling panels? If you aren't used to observing, you may have easily missed those details because when you looked up you simply noted "ceiling" in your head and no longer bothered to store its specific details in your memory.

To correct this tendency to overlook details, do the following exercise: pick a human guinea pig. Don't worry; you won't need to experiment on them (at least not with them noticing). Look at the person and try to notice 10 things about them that aren't immediately obvious. Count each detail in your head until you reach 10. For instance, you may notice that Sandra has pearl earrings, wears her wristwatch on her right wrist, doesn't wear nail polish, squints when she reads text with smaller fonts, cracks her knuckles before typing anything on her computer, and so on.

You'll see that for you to notice enough details about anyone, you'll need to slow down and take the time to observe. Becoming detail-oriented is the process of learning to maximize each moment you spend by searching for small elements in the big picture, committing them to memory, and even raising questions about the interesting details you discover.

When you ask questions about what you observe, you deepen your thinking further and start to exercise your ability to make sense of what you observe. And by adding that layer of thought to those details, you are helping yourself better commit them to memory, precisely because you've started to create a web in your mind that connects those details to a single backstory. For example, why do you think Sandra squints when she has to read fine print? Is it simply a mannerism or does she have poor eyesight? If it's the latter, why doesn't she get glasses? Repeatedly practicing such thought processes sharpens your attention to detail over time.

A writer suggests building this habit by subjecting yourself to a series of challenges. Aside from watching and noting 10 details about a specific person, you may observe a multitude of people in crowded areas (you can extend the spirit of this challenge and attempt to simply name as many details as possible about your target). Notice how they interact with one another. How many of them are chatting? How many are taking selfies? Can you spot people who're in a rush versus those who seem to be taking their sweet time?

Take field notes on one particular interaction you see; write down a detailed description and sketch out the scene, context, relationship, and overall conversation. Try to make sense of it without hearing anything they are saying—everything will be based on your observations, so you better find enough to make a coherent narrative!

Similarly, try taking a "soundwalk," an idea by Marc Weidenbaum to train your ear to listen for new things. While walking down a street, listen for specific sounds and try to locate their origin points. It's startling how much you will discover just by turning your attention to it and slowing down. It just shows you how much your attention is split. No wonder we're not as observant as we could be.

In a nod to Sherlock's purposes, you can further hone your detail-detection skills by assessing two main things when you interact with people: danger and comfort. When you come across someone, ask yourself how that person makes you feel. Say you start to notice that a man sitting across from you in a restaurant may be looking at you a little too intensely. When you get up to leave, he does the same.

He walks a little farther from behind you and you start feeling more suspicious. From the corner of your eye, you pay attention to how his hands are positioned, whether there's a bulge in his jacket that may conceal a weapon, how briskly he's walking in relation to your pace, and so on. In the face of possible danger, the ability to watch people more closely thus becomes one of necessity.

Conversely, also grab opportunities to assess for comfort. If you sense feeling comfortable with someone, even if you haven't interacted that much yet, ask yourself why. Does their manner of speaking or overall demeanor remind you of a close friend? Or maybe they're wearing an article of clothing that your favorite cousin also used to wear.

When you practice noticing how others make you feel and habitually ponder why it might be so, you'll also start picking up on details you otherwise may have missed. The important part here is to clearly articulate why you felt danger or comfort. That's where your observation skills come in, as you are giving voice to those things that were previously subconscious or even missed.

Finally, to become more detail-oriented, Klosowski suggests keeping an eye out for patterns. After all, a single observation noted one time may just be a misleading glitch instead of a truly informative detail. To get hold of details useful for decision-making and problem-solving, you'd have to observe them in a series or a composite in order to see how they relate with one another.

The process of detailed observation is like looking at the inner workings of a machine—you notice the individual cogs, but to understand how the entire machine works, you have to see each cog in relation to the other cogs. It would be hard to make any reasonable assumption from seeing just one cog. You need to see the pattern that multiple cogs create, because ultimately, you'll have to interpret each detail in the context of the entire situation you're observing instead of in a vacuum individually.

As Sherlock put it, "The little details are by far the most important." It's by noticing the little details that you get to identify the specific cogs that are causing the machine to malfunction, so to speak. In other words, the problem is more likely to be solved faster if you're keenly aware of which aspects of it to target—which cogs to repair, replace, or reposition to get the machine working again.

For example, say you need to figure out why counter transactions at a fast food restaurant you manage take more time than what's ideal for satisfactory customer service. To solve this problem, you need to observe the details of a number of transactions that happen at the counter. Are customers taking a long time to place their orders because they're having trouble seeing what's on the menu? If so, then maybe those menus need changing to improve their readability. Is the crew taking a long time to key in orders because they find the information system too confusing or tedious? Then maybe that system needs to be updated to be more user-friendly.

Do those assembling the food orders keep bumping into each other or have to navigate multiple corners just to serve up a food item? Then maybe the facility design needs improvement to be more suited to such a fast-paced setting. By observing a clear pattern, you can see the underlying causes of your problems and how to implement change. This is how you create an efficient machine instead of individually dealing with each cog as it malfunctions.

Give your 100% focus. It's already been mentioned, but proper observation demands your undivided attention. This means that if you want to thoroughly absorb the information in front of you, you should be prepared to give your 100% focus. Don't attempt to multitask and put your blinders on to ignore distractions. Distractions may come from outside of you (i.e., external distractions) or from within you (i.e., internal distractions).

External distractions may come in the form of a chatty colleague, social media or email notifications, noisy construction sounds from the other room, or uncomfortable room temperature. Internal distractions are thoughts and feelings that interfere with your ability to think and focus.

For example, you may be fretting over a recent slipup you made during an important presentation or feeling anxious about an upcoming evaluation. You may also be internally distracted by thoughts of all the other items in your to-do list, leading you to constantly worry about getting everything done and taking away your focus from the task at hand. Distractions—external or internal—all interfere with proper observation.

Thus, you need to eliminate all distractions. However, as attractive as this option may sound, it's almost always impossible to do. We live in a world of distractions, and eliminating every distracting thing isn't always an option. You can't just shoot your chatty colleague dead if he starts being a distraction, right?

So the next best thing to do is have the ability to focus despite the presence of distractions all around you. You must be able to hone your capacity for single-mindedness to the point that you can channel your full attention only on the task at hand and nothing else.

Consider the following experiment conducted by cognitive psychologists Daniel Simons and Christopher Chabris. Their 1999 study had volunteers watch a video in which two groups of people—one group dressed in white and the other in black—each pass a basketball to their own groupmates. The volunteers were instructed to count how many passes the white group made and to ignore those made by the black group. About halfway through, a person in a gorilla suit walks in and out of the video scene.

After watching the video, the volunteers were asked whether they noticed anything else other than the players in the scene. About half of them missed seeing the person in the gorilla suit. They were so focused on counting the number of basketball passes the white group made that they were blind to anything else that happened in the scene—a phenomenon known as *inattentional blindness*.

Now, while the study was meant to demonstrate a shortcoming in human attention, for our purposes, inattentional blindness is actually an advantageous thing to cultivate when you need to give your 100% focus on observing a particular phenomenon. In situations when you need to shut out distractions in order to closely observe something, it's a gift to be able to miss that gorilla walking about.

Noticing that gorilla will only distract you from correctly counting those passes. In other words, scattering your focus to notice nonessential things only takes your attention away from accurately observing what you need to observe. If you see the gorilla, you just might be subconsciously multitasking and not putting your full attention into what you should be.

Say you need to write a performance evaluation report on one of your employees, and you need to observe how he fares when it comes to following safety protocols on the production floor. To come up with an accurate observation, you need to devote your 100% focus to observing how the employee goes about his tasks on the production floor, paying keen attention to his safety practices. What should you do while you're observing? You need to put your blinders on.

Refrain from multitasking—resist the urge to check your emails on your mobile phone; avoid engaging other employees on the floor, even if you've just remembered you were wanting to talk to them; don't attempt to check on other equipment on the floor while you're there. Remember that your purpose for being there is solely to observe how a particular employee carries out safety protocols; other matters can wait until after you're done observing for performance evaluation.

It may seem obvious in that context that you must give 100% focus, but this type of attention should be emulated when you want to solve problems.

Note differences from baseline. Have you noticed how doctors assess a problem area that a patient reports to them? Say you come to your doctor complaining of back pain. Aside from asking questions about it, your doctor would likely inspect and palpate the area. How do you suppose your doctor could tell if something's not quite right with your back? Chances are, he's visually inspected and palpated enough backs in his practice that he's established a baseline of what a relatively normal back looks and feels like. For your doctor to detect whether anything's out of the ordinary, he must first have a pretty good idea of what ordinary is.

The same principle applies in the observations you attempt to do in daily life. For you to be a sharp observer, you must first know what the baseline for a person or situation is. A baseline is what is considered normal or typical for a particular object of observation. For instance, you're likely to be familiar with what is baseline behavior for a longtime buddy of yours. You're aware he's typically gregarious and loud when with crowds.

Now, at a party, he's quiet and slumped in a corner of the room. So you know something must be up, and you go to him to try to ask what's wrong. It's your knowledge of what's baseline for that particular person that allowed you to sense that something was amiss and to act accordingly to remedy the situation.

In some instances, the ability to detect when something's not quite right even becomes a matter of life and death. This is well-discussed by Jason A. Riley and Patrick Van Horne in *Left of Bang*, a book detailing the principles of the Marine Corps' Combat Hunter Program as applied to scenarios that find you on the verge of something catastrophic. The "bang" pertains to a bad event, and being "left of bang" means being at a point in time just before that bad event happens (i.e., being on the left side of that bang on a timeline).

Left of Bang is a manual that uses military situations and anecdotes to illustrate how to detect when you're about to encounter a bad event so that you can either veer away from it or prevent it from happening. While it's based on the military milieu, you can apply its principles in daily life to significantly improve the way you observe people and situations.

It advocates the importance of being sensitive to that gut feeling that "something isn't right" and of trusting your intuition so that you can avoid being entangled in unpleasant situations. It highlights the necessity of being familiar with the typical look of settings or the usual manner about people so that you can quickly detect when things have changed in a way that warrants attention or signals a potential problem.

To be adept at observation, *Left of Bang* recommends being keenly aware of "human universals," features common to all people across cultures throughout history. An example is *kinesics*, which is body language indicative of one's inner emotional state. This includes gestures, postures, and expressions of which a person may or may not be conscious but nonetheless betray what they're really feeling. Maybe someone has the habit of touching her neck when she's nervous, while another tends to purse his lips when he's angry.

Biometric cues, which are involuntary outward signs of stress such as flushed skin, dry mouth, and dilated pupils, are also worth noting. Another is *proxemics*, which pertains to space, distance, and movement. How people position and pace themselves in relation to others can reveal significant information, as in a person matching your speed as you walk along a deserted alley.

Geographics, which deals with how people behave in certain places, also offers valuable clues as to whether someone feels comfortable or ill at ease in a particular area.

Another factor worth noting is *iconography*, which encompasses visual symbols, colors, and images, such as graffiti, flags, and religious or political insignia. *Atmospherics*, which speaks of the "vibe" of an area, also offers significant observation points. For example, if the usual vibe in your office is relaxed and amiable, its sudden change to frenetic and tense could be your first clue that something's up that needs your close attention.

Training yourself to be constantly attentive to the abovementioned universals will offer you cues about what is standard for a person or environment so that you can promptly detect and respond to deviations if and when they do arise.

FBI agent LaRae Quy, drawing from 23 years of experience doing counterintelligence work, has an additional suggestion to further enhance your people-reading and observation skills.

Try to figure out a person's core personality traits and motivations. Is the person an introvert or an extrovert? Does he react to uncertainty with confrontational or avoidant behavior? Does she value the pursuit of personal significance or the preservation of social relationships? Knowing the answers to these questions will help you put a behavior you observe in the context of the individual's whole personality, thus giving you guidance on how to best interpret it.

For example, if a team member declines taking the lead on a project, it doesn't necessarily mean that she's doing so because she would rather slack off. Rather, she may be doing so because she wants to preserve her good relations with a colleague who she knows is raring to take the reins and is likely to be hostile to her if she accepted the leadership role. This plays directly into the next point about observations.

Understand people's self-perceptions. Every observation you make, especially that about people, has the potential to mean something other than it seems at face value.

For example, when you notice someone avoiding eye contact while they're answering your question, traditional body language handbooks may tell you that someone must be lying.

However, when you consider that the person you're talking to comes from a different cultural background, where avoiding eye contact is a show of respect, then that observation could mean an entirely different thing from what those handbooks suggest. For the person, his avoidance of eye contact may just be his way of showing deference to you and is thus not to be taken as a sure sign of guilt or discomfort from lying.

Hence, to make accurate observations about people, it's important for you to first understand how people perceive themselves and the situation. What is the person's worldview? What are the things they believe, the values they espouse, and the ideas they reject? How do they look at the world around them, and how do they make sense of what they see?

Consider the narratives people have about themselves and the world and examine the details and behaviors you notice in the context of those narratives. When you're aware of people's worldviews and self-perceptions, you can carry out observations at a deeper level and get to see what each of their actions really mean and why they displayed those behaviors. You'll also have a keener sense for spotting deviations from their normal ways so that you'll be guided on how to best interact with them during difficult situations.

Take for instance a supervisor's inexplicable hostility toward you. Ever since you got into the team, she seems to be always putting you down any way she can—shooting down your every idea, making sure everyone in the team knows it when you made a mistake, and making it a point that you know about her previous accomplishments and high status in the field. If you react only to those behaviors, you may retaliate by also being hostile against her, either by openly showing aggression or carrying out covert sabotage.

But if you try to dig a little deeper, you may discover that she perceives herself as the best in the business, that she values others' esteem, and that it's important to her that her superiority is not threatened by any new talent. Thus, you realize that challenging her authority will only make things worse.

You recognize that the best way to get her to stop antagonizing you is to show that you're impressed by her successes, express that you look up to her as an authority, avoid fighting over power and credit in the team, and help her realize that the work you do for the team would also benefit her reputation. Your understanding of her self-perceptions and motivations is thus the key to making the best use of your observations.

See the big picture. When the word "observation" comes up, people tend to think it's about paying close attention to the littlest details. And that's not wrong—

observation does demand an acute examination of the micro aspects of a scene, event, or person. However, people tend to forget that focusing on the details alone does not necessarily provide the complete picture.

For your observation to be truly effective and valuable, you have to observe not only the little things but the big picture as well. Otherwise, you might "fail to see the forest for the trees," leading you to make bad judgments in the end. Don't forget that observations are in support of solving specific problems or accomplishing particular goals.

Take for instance Vivian, a highly motivated manager in the middle of spearheading a new marketing campaign for the company. While Vivian has multiple inspiring plans for the said project and has drafted out every detail of what needs to be done to make it a success, she's failed to see that her individual plans put together would put a huge financial strain on the company. It turns out that the total cost of carrying out the campaign would negate any increase in profit they had hoped to gain through the marketing scheme. Hence, while Vivian was able to get all the details ironed out, she failed to see the bigger picture, leading her to make bad judgments in the end.

A combination of the micro and macro view of what's being observed is thus essential to the art of observation. Paying attention to the details is well and good, but don't forget that it's just half the story. Zoom out and observe the bigger picture as well, noting how the details fit together to give you the right information you need to achieve gain and avoid losses.

When you do observation right, you'll be able to gather so much information about the problem or situation. You'll have a myriad of details about the what, where, when, who, why, and how. The next question is, what are you to do with that mass of information at your disposal?

You'll need to be able to organize and make sense of the information, connect it with other pieces of information in meaningful ways, and form a coherent narrative using them all together. How you're going to do just that is answered in the next section— by learning the art of deductive reasoning. This is how you make use of the information you've now observed.

Deductive Reasoning

You've probably seen it happen—a super-detective like Sherlock Holmes arriving at a scene and then immediately knowing what happened just by looking at the area. There's a cascade of scenes that flash in his mind, telling a story of the series of events that must've happened that led to the specific arrangement and state of things in the area. He has taken a wide range of observations and immediately formed the story that led to them all. How'd he do it?

The answer is by deductive reasoning. Now, while the way Sherlock Holmes goes about it makes the whole thing seem more like a superpower than a human faculty, deductive reasoning is something you're capable of as well. In fact, you do it on a daily basis.

Say you arrive home and find a puddle of water on the kitchen floor. From that piece of information, you try to backtrack to what must've happened that caused that puddle to be there. You note location (e.g., is it near the sink or underneath a leaky roof area?), amount and quality of the water (e.g., does it look like clean drinking water or does it have a murky quality?), and surrounding objects (e.g., are there broken shards of drinking glass nearby or perhaps a toppled fishbowl?).

You then use such information to reason backward from the effect you're seeing (i.e., the puddle of water), to the most probable cause based on the details you observe (i.e., someone knocked over a drinking glass). You've just performed deduction.

Deduction is essentially *reverse storytelling*. It's the art of taking the information available to you at a given moment and then reasoning backward from effect to cause.

Deductive reasoning is thus an essential skill to master when it comes to problem-solving. Deduction is what allows you to make reasonable assumptions about the causes of events and thus enables you to solve problems at their roots.

Would you really get someone to look for and patch holes in your roof when you've studied the situation and figured out that the true cause for that puddle was a dropped drinking glass and not a leaky roof?

If you want to hone your powers of deduction, there are a number of techniques you can practice. The following section outlines five of the best ways you can go about it: (1) make a fishbone diagram, (2) practice coming up with potential causes for details you observe, (3) watch people and deduce the conversations they're having, (4) talk out loud, and (5) put aside your ego to become more open-minded.

Each of these techniques will help you make sense of all the information you've gathered through the strategies of observation discussed in the previous section. In the process of becoming a master problem-solver, you need to be able to not only observe keenly, but also make sense of those observations sensibly.

Make a fishbone diagram. A fishbone diagram is a method that allows you to identify multiple potential causes for a problem or an effect. Being able to infer causes based on an observed effect is an integral aspect of deduction, especially when it comes to problem-solving. Fleshing out a list of all the possible causes of a problem simultaneously provides you with a blueprint of the specific factors you need to focus on to ultimately find viable solutions.

The fishbone diagram is so structured that those causes are placed in categories, so you get a more orderly perspective of the entire situation. It's a more organized way of working in reverse from effect to cause and is a frequently used tool for structuring brainstorming sessions. The end product is a visual display of all the factors—both from a micro and a macro perspective—that play a role in leading to the effect or the problem.

To make a fishbone diagram, first write a problem statement or effect somewhere in the middle right portion of a whiteboard or any writing surface you've chosen. Draw a box around it, then a horizontal line across the page that ends in that problem box. That box will serve as the "head" of the fishbone.

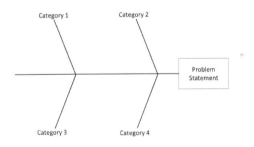

Next, draw the "bones" of the body by sketching widely spaced vertical lines that come out of the main horizontal line. Draw bones above and below the main line, slightly slanting away from the head of the fishbone. These bones will be labeled with the different categories of the causes you come up with. It's up to you to name the categories that apply to the problem you're working on.

Every time you come up with a possible cause for the problem, write it down as a connection to the particular "bone" it's categorized under. You can write the same cause under multiple categories if applicable. Then, for each noted cause, continue asking what might've caused it, and write it down as a connection to that cause, and so on until you can no longer think of a more primary cause. This will allow you to exercise your deductive reasoning skills until you arrive at the most fundamental root causes of the problem.

When you're done with the diagram, scrutinize the causes you've listed and consider the evidence regarding it. How much does the identified cause really contribute to creating the effect? Is its link with the problem well-established and significant enough to consider seriously? Get into the habit of thinking, "What would make this cause a true and significant factor in the problem at hand?"

For example, say you're a hotel manager trying to understand the causes of low customer satisfaction ratings for your hotel service. Write the problem in a box as the fishbone "head" and the categories of possible causes (in this case, the four P's of service industries) as the main "bones." Doing this, the initial stages of your fishbone diagram would look like so:

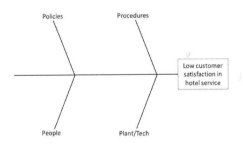

Then start filling in each category with possible causes. For example, you've identified that possible causes for the problem are (1) the slow resolution of customer complaints and (2) the hotel staff's inability to be sensitive to the customers' needs, thus leading the customer to be dissatisfied with the service.

Asking yourself why your staff may lack sensitivity to customer needs, you may consider that they work such long hours that they are reduced to providing just the bare minimum of service; they no longer have energy enough to pay more attention to customers' more specific needs. Given that, your fishbone diagram would now indicate the following:

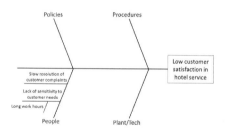

Continuing the process of asking yourself why the problem exists, you start identifying more possible causes and noting them under the given categories, leading your diagram to look something like this:

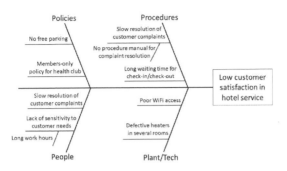

By systematically working backward from the problem to the causes, you get to identify specific aspects of your situation that you can then address accordingly. The fishbone diagram is a tool that effectively focuses your efforts to solve the problem at its roots—or, in this case, at its bones.

It's a great way to guide your thinking in the process of reverse storytelling, as it allows you to concretely trace how the problem is linked back to specific causative factors. Think of the fishbone diagram as a scaffold that helps you build up your deductive reasoning and problem-solving skills more effectively.

Note details and potential causes. Remember how one technique to sharpen your observation skills involves watching a person or a scene and noting 10 details about it? You can do a "level-up" of this technique in order to develop your deductive reasoning. This exercise involves taking a scene, a person, or any other thing, and observing 10 details about it. Then, for each of those details, write down five possible causes that may have led that particular detail to be the way it is. Try to vary the potential causes you list down, ranging from the plainly realistic to the downright bizarre. This will train your ability to create a story around every detail, thus exercising your skills in reverse storytelling, which is what deductive reasoning is about.

Say you've decided to observe your neighborhood park. You note several details about it: five benches, three joggers circling the area, two kids on the seesaw, a child enjoying an ice cream cone, a man sweeping dead leaves from under a tree, a broken swing, a lunch basket abandoned by a bench, a sign supposed to say "park" but missing the letter P, a woman reading under a shade, and a large tree branch lying in the middle of a footpath.

You then take one of those details—for instance, the large tree branch on the footpath—and try to come up with five backstories explaining why the branch is there. One, the branch may have simply fallen off a tree because a huge gust of wind had knocked it off. Two, the branch may have been infected by insects and was thus hacked off by park caretakers to save the tree. Three, it may have fallen off a load of branches someone was transporting on the way to a bonfire.

Four, a group of mischievous kids may have purposefully dragged the branch to the middle of the path to trip people passing through. And five, the branch may have been placed there by a secret agent as a coded message to signify a meeting place. By trying to determine the possible causes of what you're seeing, you're exercising your deductive powers.

Practice people-watching to deduce conversation content. This is another upgraded exercise from your observation-sharpening set of techniques. When you observe people, select those engaged in a conversation you can't hear, then deduce what they might be talking about. What might be the relationship between those people? What is each of them saying, and what is the other's response? What might be their motivations behind the things they're saying?

An interesting way to do this is to use book or TV characters. Witnessing a particular action or decision a character has made, try to deduce what might've led them to act or decide the way they did. Alternatively, you may watch a sitcom on mute or watch a foreign movie without subtitles. Figure out what the characters are saying to each other and state your reasons for your assumptions. You may also try to come up with two opposing stories for each scenario, then pick the story that's more likely to be true. Explain why the story you've chosen is the more sensible one, using evidence you've observed in the scene.

Say you watch a scene in which a woman is talking to a fruit vendor stationed in a food stall by the street. The woman is holding some dollar bills, while the vendor appears to be picking out fruits to offer the woman. They talk a bit more, and then the woman gives the bills to the vendor but refuses to take the fruits in exchange. The vendor smiles as the woman walks away.

What might've they said to each other during that interaction? Why did the woman give the vendor money without taking the fruits in exchange? From that, you could then deduce a number of stories. Maybe the woman was doing an act of charity. Or maybe the woman personally knew the vendor and was paying off a debt. Or maybe they agreed that the woman would just pick up the fruits later, after she's done with an errand. Running such stories in your head will train your mind to get into the habit of deduction.

Talk out loud. When you're trying to solve problems, it's natural that you engage in a process of thinking. But during this process, do you also have moments when you're thinking about the way you're thinking? The act of thinking about your own thinking is known as metacognition.

In recent years, problem-solving has come to be considered in light of metacognition, and for good reason—metacognition allows you to detect errors in your own deductive problem-solving methods and continually check yourself for faulty reasoning so that you avoid making errors in judgment. Enhancing your metacognitive skills is thus a powerful way to sharpen your powers of deduction and problem-solving.

So how do you enhance your metacognition? The experts recommend this technique: talk out loud. The effectiveness of this method for improving problem-solving is backed by a study published by the University of Arkansas in 2011. The study looked closely into a teaching/learning strategy known as Talking Aloud Partner Problem-Solving (TAPPS), in which two people are partnered: one is tasked to solve a problem (i.e., the problem-solver), while the other (i.e., the monitor) is instructed to just listen, refrain from giving advice, and monitor the comments of the problem-solver while encouraging him to notice his own thinking pattern.

The researchers found that what actually improved the problem-solving process wasn't the monitor but the problem-solver's own act of thinking aloud. By talking out loud, the problem-solver engages in metacognition. He's forced to put his line of reasoning in words and hear them too, thus allowing him to detect the lack of logical connections or insufficient evidence for certain assumptions. Thus, if you want to sharpen your own skills in deduction and problem-solving, you need to practice thinking out loud, whether with a partner or just by yourself.

Say you need to figure out how to increase the low number of attendees who've signed up for an upcoming seminar you've organized for startup entrepreneurs. Talking aloud to yourself, you may say,

"Why isn't there more people signing up to attend this seminar? Maybe they're just not interested in the topic. But this topic is relevant and would surely be helpful for those who're currently into or even just planning to enter startup entrepreneurship. If it's relevant and helpful, then the problem isn't the topic. Maybe info about this seminar has just failed reached the people who would consider it relevant and helpful. So one way to attract more attendees would be to have a more targeted marketing campaign. I should come up with a list of all startup businesses in the area and reach out to them specifically and talk to them about this seminar. Posting info about this on social media sites for entrepreneurs might also help."

Put your ego aside. While it's tempting to think that the ability for deductive reasoning relies mainly on intellect—having the cognitive capacity to use logic in order to arrive at a fairly certain conclusion—it's important to recognize that it also calls for certain noncognitive skills: personal qualities and attitudes that have less to do with smarts and more to do with character. One of the most basic attitudes essential to developing a keen sense of deductive reasoning is humility.

Humility involves having the capacity to put your ego aside and to steer clear from having a self-important perspective. In connection with deductive reasoning, it involves the willingness to backtrack on your initial assumptions, reconsider them with an open mind, and, if the situation calls for it, admit you were wrong. Only with humility can you look at the information and evidence in front of you with honesty and clarity, free from your own personal biases that tend to distort such information to cater to selfish needs.

Having too big an ego will only lead you to force the facts to fit whatever theory you've originally made up in your mind, because lack of humility can compel you to do whatever it takes to avoid showing any shortcoming on your part. An inflated ego can get in the way of seeing the facts as they are and allowing them to shape and reshape the theory, and not the other way around. Oftentimes, we want a specific outcome and will interpret all the evidence to support that outcome. Ego does not promote effective problem-solving.

Humility is thus what enables you to be flexible enough to respond to the evidence you discover in a way that does not distort the assumptions you end up making. Interestingly, the subjugation of women throughout history has shaped this quality in them more effectively. Delving into stereotypes, women needed to have the capacity to accommodate others as well as be flexible enough to adjust to the situation in order to avoid or pacify conflict. The masculine way, on the other hand, valued power and dominance over flexibility and adaptation.

Confronted with something that goes against their beliefs and assumptions, the masculine way of responding was one of either defensiveness or aggression instead of accommodation. Seeking others' wisdom and taking critical feedback are considered signs of weakness and are thus avoided by masculine personalities with strong egos. Humble people, on the other hand, are more readily receptive to new information and evidence, even if it counters their initial assumptions. This grants them the ability to make decisions based on actual data and arrive at conclusions truly derived from the evidence at hand.

Take for instance Jerry, an entrepreneur who runs an online clothing store. He's run into a problem—an angry rant from an unsatisfied customer has gone viral online. His ego hurt, Jerry reacts impulsively and posts an angry reply to the customer. The whole thing blows up and Jerry starts receiving cancellations for orders left and right.

Fearing the disintegration of his business, Jerry tries to calm down and investigate the situation more closely. Upon humbly reaching out to the customer and finding her complaints well-founded, Jerry apologizes and promptly sends in a product replacement with a freebie to boot. Satisfied with the resolution, the customer posts a public appreciation of how Jerry's store effectively handled her complaint. By setting aside his ego, Jerry was able to correct his assumptions and target the cause of the problem, leading to its eventual resolution.

As another example, say you belong to one of three groups each given a hula hoop. There's a big pile of about 30 plastic balls in your midst. The challenge is to put all 30 balls within your group's own hula hoop. If everyone simply lets their ego take charge, all three groups would fight over getting the balls for themselves and make it unlikely for any single group to succeed.

But setting your ego aside will allow you to reconsider the situation and use your reason with better clarity. Why not have all three hula hoops encircle the pile of 30 balls? That way, all groups accomplish the goal. The resolution was made possible only by allowing your clarity of reason to transcend the selfish need to be the only one who "wins."

So there you have it—all the techniques, tips, and tricks you need to master the art of using observation and deductive reasoning toward effective problem-solving.

Observation, when done correctly, allows you to gather every bit of information you need to know in order to solve a problem. You can improve your observation skills by becoming more detail-oriented, devoting your 100% focus, being alert to deviations from the baseline, having insight into people's self-perceptions, and seeing how the details fit into the big picture.

Deductive reasoning is what turns the information you gathered from observing into significant assumptions, conclusions, and judgments. By becoming proficient at deducing, you get to use the evidence in front of you as breadcrumbs that lead to the root causes of a problem, which you can then address more effectively. Using the fishbone diagram, enumerating potential causes of every detail you observe, practicing people-watching to deduce conversations talking out loud, and putting aside your ego to be more open-minded are all essential techniques to help you achieve expert-level deductive reasoning.

Who knows? Given enough time and practice, you might just be the one to personify a real-life Sherlock Holmes, solving the most mystifying of your workplace enigmas by your sheer powers of observation and deduction.

Takeaways:

- A key element of Sherlock's problem-solving abilities is the ability to use information—specifically, taking in and absorbing information and then connecting the dots and making deductions and hypotheses based on that information. We all look at the same situations, yet some of us come away with completely different conclusions. That's because of what is done with the information in (1) observations and (2) deductions.

- Observations are all about taking in information. The truth is, we really aren't very observant in our daily lives. You probably don't know the color of the ceiling or floor in the room you are currently in. Becoming better at observations helps your problem-solving because that's where your solutions will come from.

- You can focus on becoming more detail-oriented, devoting 100% of your focus and attention, paying attention to the baseline of people and situations, understanding people's self-perceptions, and taking a look at the big picture and not getting lost in the details.

- Deductions are about connecting the dots and explaining what's in front of you. Deductions are essentially storytelling in reverse. You can accomplish this by learning the fishbone method of naming causes and motivations, training yourself to think through cause and effect, watching people and trying to assign a narrative or story to an interaction, talking out loud, and putting ego aside to allow yourself to explore solutions and reasons that are against your beliefs.

Chapter 4. Shift Your Perspective

You've probably heard of the old adage that says a well-defined problem already takes you halfway toward finding the solution. Certainly, there's truth to that. Much of the problem-solving process relies on the statement of the problem itself, as it demonstrates understanding of what the core issue is and at the same time reflects the focus and perspective you're taking as you attempt to look for answers. Shifting your perspective *is* defining and refining the problem.

This is why the art of sharpening your problem-solving skills would need you to not only practice how to find solutions, but also hone your ability to state and restate problems in ways that will serve as fertile ground for the growth of novel ideas and solutions. You'll need to learn how to consider problems from different perspectives, reimagine and challenge the realities of the world as you know it, and adapt ways of thinking you might not have previously attempted.

If it helps, you can think of this as an extension of previous chapters and thinking creatively about solutions for problems. It's just another way to get the resolution you are seeking.

Simply continuing to look at a problem or a situation in the same way each time only leads to tired old ideas that don't really offer much in terms of actually resolving a tricky situation. To break free from such limiting molds, you'll need to get past your own biases, opinions, perspectives, and experiences and learn how to expand your worldview to gain a full understanding of what you need to tackle what's in front of you.

Say that your company needs to cut energy costs, so it has recently adopted a new energy-saving policy that requires employees to follow measures such as making sure lights in rooms not used are turned off, computers not in use are shut down or put in hibernate mode, and the air-conditioning unit is turned off once the clock strikes 5:00 p.m. As a manager, you've been assigned to oversee this policy's implementation. However, it soon becomes apparent that employees are not complying with these energy-saving measures.

You've tried everything you can to try to modify employees' behaviors, such as by offering incentives, conducting meetings, posting reminders, holding seminars, and even imposing sanctions, but to no avail. The problem remains unsolved, and your company's energy expenses have remained the same, if not increased.

Now, if you were to try to solve that problem by simply intensifying your efforts at modifying employee behavior, you might not accomplish much. The thing is, you've been trying to address the situation from a single perspective: that energy costs could be reduced only by changing how employees behave.

How about shifting your perspective by redefining the problem?

Try to look past the narrow view that only trying to control employee behaviors would have the effect of cutting energy costs. For instance, you may redefine the problem not as a human resource issue but as an engineering or industrial concern. Seeing the problem this way may then have you look into engineering solutions that would implement energy-saving measures without needing human actions in the process, such as automatic shutdown of company appliances at preset times.

Or maybe you could check out replacing your light and air conditioning units with those that have better energy-saving features. You may even consider subscribing to a different, cheaper energy source that may be available in your area.

Moreover, you may redefine the problem by redirecting its focus. Instead of focusing only on how your company can cut energy costs, how about brainstorming how you can generate more earnings to help pay for those energy expenses? This change in perspective will help you address the issue in more than one way and open up more diverse and innovative solutions for you to implement.

Redefining problems is just one of the strategies this chapter will discuss to help you shift your perspective toward coming up with creative and effective solutions. In this chapter, you'll learn the significance and practical applications of changing perspective not only by restating problems, but also by such strategies as imagining hypotheticals, creating psychological distance, thinking laterally, thought experiments, and thinking through wearing six hats.

Redefining and Rephrasing Problems

One of the most direct and effective ways you can shift your perspective about a problem is by redefining or rephrasing the issue in front of you.

You may have been going around in circles, listing redundant ideas in trying to solve X. In reality, you can redefine the problem to focus on Y or Z, the solution for which then having the secondary effect of solving X as well. While you may be working with the same data set or information all across the board, redefining the issue as X, Y, or Z puts a fresh spin on it and allows you to see the same information through different lenses. Such redefinition allows you either a wider or a more unique set of potential solutions for what you're currently tackling.

To facilitate this type of thinking, there are a number of specific techniques you can employ to redefine and rephrase your problem: invert, paraphrase, redirect the focus, vary the stress pattern, and substitute.

Invert problems. In stating problems, it's common to pose the question such that the answer is all about what you need to do to achieve a positive outcome. For example, you may ask "What do I need to do to be a better manager?" or "How should I behave as an employee if I want to succeed in my career?"

As noble as the intentions behind these phrasings are, they have been asked and considered so many times in the same way that the answers you come up with may just be taking you halfway forward instead of allowing you to come up with better, more varied solutions—solutions that are innovative and unique enough to set you apart from the rest and propel you toward better outcomes. So to spice up the menu of ideas you come up with, try an altogether different way of stating the problem: invert it.

Carl Jacobi, a German mathematician, was known for utilizing such an approach to solve hard problems. Following a strategy of *man muss immer umkehren*, or "invert, always invert," Jacobi would write down math problems in inverse form and find that it was easier for him to arrive at the solution that way. Applying this inverse way of thinking to a different life area, billionaire investor Charlie Munger challenges the youth to ponder on the inverse of success instead of simply focusing on how to achieve success.

He poses the question, "What do you want to avoid?" and offers a likely response: sloth and unreliability. These qualities are roadblocks to success, and you get to shine a spotlight on them precisely by asking why people fail instead of why they succeed. By inverting the question of success, you get to discover drivers of failure and are thus able to avoid such behaviors in order to improve.

So instead of asking what you need to do to be a better manager, try considering what a terrible manager would do. If your business model centers on innovation, ask "How could we limit this company's innovative potentials?" If you're looking to improve your productivity, ask "What are the things I do to distract myself?" Generally, instead of asking "How do I solve this problem," ask "How would I *cause* this problem?"

This is also known as *reverse brainstorming*, a process whereby you consider an inverted or negative question and allow the answers to simply flow out. Other questions for reverse brainstorming may include asking how a project can fail, what the worst thing about a product is, and how a process could be made slower and more expensive. Use the answers to these inverted questions as guidelines on what to avoid.

The art of inverting questions and reverse brainstorming is a powerful thinking tool, as it shines a light not only on which paths to take but often more importantly on which paths to steer clear of or guard against.

Moreover, inversion allows you the unique opportunity to consider both sides of an issue instead of simply succumbing to how you've always perceived things or what your belief system has dictated since forever. All too often, particular patterns of thinking have been so ingrained in you that you fail to see it when they no longer apply to the present situation.

By forcing you to first look into both sides of an argument, much like a jury would in a court of law, inversion helps you consider even evidence that challenges your own beliefs and disconfirms your initial conclusions. This makes your problem-solving process more reliable and objective so that you get to a solution that's truly effective at targeting the core issues.

Paraphrase. Paraphrasing is a method of restating problems by using different words to deliver the same thought. Proposed by Morgan D. Jones in his book *The Thinker's Toolkit: 14 Powerful Techniques for Problem Solving*, paraphrasing is basically about rewording a question without losing its original meaning. For example, if the original statement asks "How can we increase the sales of Product X?" a paraphrased version may ask "How do we get more people to buy Product X?"

Pondering the same set of words over and over again is only bound to numb your brain and dull it from coming up with fresh ideas. By stimulating your brain to think of the same problem in different terms, paraphrasing refreshes your thinking and opens up your mind to solutions that would've stayed hidden from you otherwise. Even a slight change of vocabulary may spark a solution to your woes based on context, personal history, experience, connotation, or implication.

Redirect the focus. Another method included in Jones's *Thinker's Toolkit* is redirecting the focus. For this method, you'll need to proactively seek out a different focus, distinct but still related to the problem. For instance, if your original question goes "How can we increase product sales?" you may redirect the focus by asking "How can we decrease production costs?"

Another example would be if your initial problem statement asks "How do we recycle plastic waste in our company?" A redirected focus may instead ask "How do we prevent people from using plastic in our company?" These are ways of solving the same problem, but by focusing on a different solution.

Redirecting the focus helps you broaden your view while tackling an issue so that you're not boxed in a single line of thinking and instead are forced to consider alternative solutions. It helps you address the same general concern in a more comprehensive and well-rounded way, thus also broadening the impact of the solutions you ultimately come up with.

Vary the stress pattern. Suggested by H. Scott Fogler and Steven E. LeBlanc in their book *Strategies for Creative Problem Solving*, this method involves looking at the same problem statement but varying which words or phrases you place the emphasis on. Maybe you've heard communication gurus advise you about noting how people put the stresses on the words in a sentence, as this is likely to give insight on what the speaker is really saying.

For instance, one who says "I did not steal his wallet" with the stress on "I" may suggest that the speaker knows someone else stole the wallet. If the stress is placed on "steal," the speaker could be suggesting that they may not have stolen the wallet but have done something else with it. Just by varying where the emphasis is placed, the same statement gets to mean different things.

Adapting the above concept to problem-solving, varying the stress patterns in a problem statement could lead to interesting insights on how to tackle the issue at hand. Consider the problem statement "Hotel guests are not satisfied with the quality and speed of housekeeping services." If you place the emphasis on "hotel guests," you may consider the question "Are all hotel guests unsatisfied with the service or just a subset of them? If it's the latter, who are those that are typically unsatisfied and what are their specific experiences that led them to that evaluation?"

Alternatively, you may put the stress on "quality" and ask how to upgrade the quality of services delivered. If you place the emphasis on "speed," you may then consider how to improve the promptness of housekeeping services.

Ultimately, varying the stress patterns of the problem statement allows you to reflect on different aspects of the issue and break it down into more manageable chunks for targeted solution-finding.

Substitute. Another of the strategies suggested by Fogler and LeBlanc, substituting is done by replacing certain terms in the problem statement with their explicit definitions. Substituting works best when you need to restate a problem in such a way as to create a more concrete scenario for you and your brainstorming team to visualize. When you substitute words that create a picture or scene you can easily imagine, you'll find that solutions are likely to occur to you more naturally as well.

For example, take the same problem statement above and substitute the phrase "housekeeping services" with its explicit definition. Doing so, you may come up with a problem that goes "Hotel guests are not satisfied with the quality and speed of how their rooms are cleaned and how they are provided with necessities such as glassware, towels, and toiletries."

This creates a picture in your mind about the specific tasks that need to be improved in terms of quality and speed. It leads you to come up with such ideas as informing your staff about target duration and other standards of performance when it comes to cleaning rooms and implementing a better system by which your guests can let your staff know about their needs.

Redefining and rephrasing problems is an important and valuable tool that enables you to take the same information and see it through a different lens. Whether by inversion, paraphrasing, redirection of focus, varying of stress patterns, or substitution, restating the problem will allow you to shift your perspective in such a way that will clear the path toward finding fresh and ingenious solutions.

Imagining Hypotheticals

"What if humans were capable of flying?"
"What if the polio vaccine was never developed?"
"What if the world's landmasses never broke up into separate continents and instead remained as Pangaea to this day?"

The above questions are examples of hypotheticals, "what if" questions that tickle your mind into thinking from other perspectives and challenge you to question your premises. Imagining hypotheticals goes beyond simple thinking skills that require only memorization, description of an observable event or situation, or even analysis of facts and concrete events. Because hypotheticals pose questions about what isn't, what hasn't happened, or what isn't likely to ever happen, they challenge the imagination in new ways and sharpen creative thinking and practical intelligence.

For instance, you've never considered the implications of human flight because it's impossible, so there is a world of thoughts that have remained unexplored. For instance, how would traffic lights work, what kind of licensing process would be required, would we still have cars and airplanes, and how would safety work? Now, how would those rules and laws apply to normal traffic situations in the present day?

And such are precisely the kind of higher-order thinking skills that education systems need to develop, campaigns Robert Sternberg, a leading cognitive psychologist. Sternberg argues that students need to be taught not just how to read, memorize facts, or describe current phenomena but, more importantly, how to think effectively—and one valuable way such can be done is by pondering over hypotheticals.

For example, instead of just having your brainstorming team consider the question, "What logo design would attract more customers?" you may challenge them with, "What if you're allowed to use only black and white, how would you design a striking company logo?" Trying to answer "what if" questions hones your problem-solving skills by stretching your mind to consider everything from the unlikely to the impossible, thus opening you up to a more diverse world of alternative explanations and solutions.

An interesting way to apply this technique to problem situations is to consider scenarios in which certain conventional elements are either elevated, missing, or rendered unavailable. To trigger solutions to such novel problems, you'll need to reimagine their elements so as to create new hypothetical versions that would be easier to solve.

For example, try working out a solution by imagining the barriers you encounter being lifted one by one. At some point, a new version of the problem that emerges out of doing so is likely to resemble a situation you've already resolved in the past. Upon encountering such a situation, your mind will then be able to fire out a number of solutions, one or more of which may work for your reimagined problem. If your solution for that reimagined problem is untypical of the solutions for your original problem, then you've just come up with an innovation.

Suppose the problem situation is needing to exit a room. The conventional ways to do so are to walk out of the door or jump out of the window. But what if the door is blocked by a raging fire and the room is on the 10th-floor of the building? These conditions have now rendered your conventional solutions fatal. You can only get out of the room either by finding a way to kill that fire or by having the capacity to survive a fall of several hundred feet.

To find a solution, you now need to think of the other available elements in unconventional ways. You consider the curtains hanging by the window, and then it hits you—you may be able to survive a jump from that 10th-floor window if you had a parachute made out of those curtains.

Thus, you have now transformed the situation into a question of how to make a parachute out of window curtains. By redefining a seemingly insurmountable problem until it becomes a task for which you can apply an old solution, you were thus able to think up innovations that are not only more interesting, but also more practical.

Applied in the work arena, consider how this might help solve a problem of how to present your company's research data and products in the most engaging way possible for your consumers. The conventional solution to this may be to provide flyers that introduce your products and state your message clearly using well-crafted text.

But imagine if your consumers were an alien species that doesn't understand letters and words the way humans do. How would you present your product information then? Introducing this hypothetical element has made conventional solutions to the problem useless, so you're forced to consider alternative ways to get your message across. This opens your mind up to the possibility of using advertising campaigns that present interesting images instead of words or that engage your consumers' auditory or even tactile senses.

Hypothetical situations taken to the extreme are thought experiments, and Albert Einstein in particular was known to use these. He called them *gedankenexperiments*, which is German for "thought experiment."

A thought experiment, in a more general context, is essentially playing out a "what if" scenario to its end. It's acting as if a theory or hypothesis was true, diving deep into the ramifications, and seeing what happens to your "what if" scenario under intense scrutiny. A thought experiment allows you to analyze interesting premises you could never do in reality and make new leaps of logic and discovery because you can analyze premises that current knowledge doesn't yet reach

For example, one of the most famous thought experiments is called *Schrödinger's cat*, which was first proposed by physicist Erwin Schrödinger.

In his thought experiment, he sealed a cat inside a box along with two things: a radioactive element and a vial of poison. There is a 50% chance that the radioactive element will decay over the hour, and if it does, then the poison will be released automatically to kill the cat.

But in the 50% chance the radioactive element does not decay, the cat will remain alive. Because of the equal probabilities, it was argued that the cat was simultaneously alive and dead in the box. Without getting into the weeds too much, this is a clear paradox because it is impossible for something to be in two different states simultaneously, being dependent on a random molecular event that wasn't sure to occur.

In other words, the Schrödinger's cat thought experiment proved that there were constraints of current quantum physics theories and certainly gaps in the knowledge of how they were to be applied. This never could have been something observable or testable, and a simple thought experiment was able to discover it.

Thought experiments were one of Einstein's superpowers. He could imagine a scenario, play it out mentally with shocking accuracy and detail, then extract the subtle conclusions that laid within.

One of Einstein's most famous *gedankenexperiments* begins with a simple premise: what would happen if you chase and then eventually caught up and rode a beam of light through space? In theory, once you caught up to the beam of light, it would appear to be frozen next to you because you are moving at the same speed. Just like if you are walking at the same pace as a car driving next to you, there is no acceleration so the car would appear to be stuck to your side.

The only problem was that this was an impossible proposition at the turn of the century. If you catch up to the light and the light appears to be frozen right next to you, then it is inherently impossible to be light. It ceases to be light at that moment. This means one of the rules of physics were broken or disproved with this elementary thought.

Therefore, one of the assumptions that underlay physics at the time had to change, and Einstein realized that the assumption of time as a constant had to change. This directly laid the path for relativity. The closer you get to the speed the light, the more time becomes different for you— relative to your speed of travel.

This thought experiment allowed Einstein to challenge the convention and eventually challenge what was thought to be set-in-stone rules set forth by Isaac Newton's three laws of energy and matter. This thought experiment was instrumental in realizing that people should have questioned old models and fundamental "rules" instead of trying to conform their theories to them.

Taking an Entirely Different Viewpoint

While restating problems and imagining hypotheticals to their logical conclusion are effective methods of tweaking your thinking toward good solutions, sometimes you need something more radical to push you toward fresh ideas and innovative resolutions. So to add to your toolbox of problem-solving devices, what follows are some strategies to help you take an entirely different viewpoint on the problem you're facing.

Psychological distance. Trying to solve a problem, especially when you've been grappling with it for a considerable amount of time already, is bound to be exhausting and emotionally draining. You may start to feel stressed, frustrated, or at times overly excited, especially when you're personally invested in the outcome. When this happens, chances are you won't be able to think as clearly or creatively as you can. This is where the necessity of creating psychological distance comes in.

Creating psychological distance means giving yourself some distance from the problem so that you can trigger fresh ways of tackling it. One way to create such distance is by imagining that you're solving the problem for someone else rather than for yourself. Think about how good you are at giving life advice to someone else or how easy it is to offer dating advice to a friend, while you yourself typically agonize over your personal life and love dilemmas to no end.

In the same way, thinking of a problem as someone else's rather than your own can help give you that break from the emotional involvement or cognitive pressure that blocks your ability to think objectively and creatively about the situation.

Imagine you're working with a colleague who you suspect is gossiping about you behind your back and sabotaging your project ideas. If you try to resolve the situation based only on what you would personally want to do, you may react based on your strongly negative emotions alone and end up causing a scene in the office or behave in a passive-aggressive manner, compromising the productivity of the entire team.

To resolve that relational problem, it would help if you think of it as happening to someone else. Consider every remark and action of your colleague as something you're observing being done to another person rather than to you. This psychological distance will help you minimize the emotional strain you have with regard to feeling personally attacked.

Who knows? You may end up seeing how those remarks and actions are harmless after all. If nothing else, you'll get to consider what the appropriate way of dealing with the situation would be.

Imagine what would make you admire the way the other person responds to the conflict situation, then use it as a model for your own behavior.

Alternatively, you may create psychological distance by imagining how you might solve the problem if you come across it five years into the future rather than right now. You may also think about how someone on the other side of the world might be conceptualizing the same problem and how differently their approach might go in trying to solve it. These strategies not only help take the pressure off, but also allow you to focus on the more universal, abstract parts of the situation that you may otherwise miss.

After you've looked at the problem from a distance, though, it's important to zoom back in on its details. This is an important step because reimagining a problem in the context of a different person, time, or place may reveal useful universal themes but have variations in terms of the little things that make that problem unique to your specific situation.

For instance, while you may imagine a sophisticated, high-tech solution to an industrial problem when you consider how it might be solved five years from now, that particular solution may not yet be available in the current scene. Thus, you need only get a general inspiration from that imagined future solution, then look at specific details in your present situation that may make it possible to apply a modified version of that solution.

Another technique by which you can create psychological distance is by zooming out enough to be able to incorporate ideas from other fields when considering your problem. Pulling knowledge and solutions from other fields—even seemingly unrelated ones—offers an entirely new world of possibilities to consider. A conventional idea in one field has the potential of being an extraordinary innovation in a different field, if applied in the right way. Of course, this is intentionally engaging in what combinatory play creates.

The advantages offered by pulling together knowledge and resources from multiple disciplines to aid problem-solving are evident in the findings of researcher and professor Brian Uzzi. Analyzing over 26 million scientific papers published over the last several centuries, Professor Uzzi found that the most impactful have been those done by teams with members coming from an atypical combination of backgrounds. Another investigation he conducted also revealed that top-performing studies cited an atypical combination of other studies, often pulling in at least 10% of their citations from fields other than their own.

Clearly, combining knowledge from different areas, especially those not typically thought of as going together, is beneficial for the conception of effective solutions and successful ideas.

Real-world solutions that have been the fruits of fusing knowledge from different disciplines include the development of the robotic doctor. Robotic doctors have been developed for such purposes as assessing patients, assisting in surgeries, and remotely delivering medical services. Knowledge and skills from a combination of different fields—including medicine, biology, physics, engineering, and computer science—had to be pooled together to make this groundbreaking and impactful innovation possible.

By creating psychological distance and reimagining problems in the context of a different time, place, or field, innovators can truly push the frontiers of what is possible when it comes to finding solutions.

Lateral thinking. When trying to solve problems, traditional methods suggest using a series of steps, undertaken in the right sequence and based on logic, in order to arrive at a single correct solution. While this "vertical thinking" may be effective in certain situations, other domains require a different kind of thinking that will need you to move not vertically through a series of steps but crossways in a sort of expansive and counterintuitive way. This latter type of thinking is what's known as "lateral thinking."

While vertical thinking is all about analyzing known rules, facts, and widely held preconceptions about a phenomenon, lateral thinking involves shattering those preconceptions and suspending widely held beliefs while looking for a solution. To think laterally is to be prepared to jump randomly among unrelated thoughts and to work with ideas that may appear odd or wrong at first.

By allowing your mind to break free of the rigid conditions of logic and rational problem-solving, lateral thinking leads you to paths toward breakthroughs and fresh solutions. For example, while vertical thinking would have you get to the exit point of a maze by going through the twists and turns within it, lateral thinking might simply have you go around the wall of the maze to get to the exit point nonetheless.

In his book *Lateral Thinking*, author and creative thought pioneer Edward de Bono explains that this manner of thinking is all about breaking boundaries and smashing conventions to come up with something original. This is essentially how lateral thinking differs from redefining problems and imagining hypotheticals. While both redefinition and hypotheticals seek to reimagine or rearrange existing elements in the problem, de Bono says that lateral thinking aims to change those very elements.

To help you develop this mindset, de Bono offers the following techniques: using an analogy, reversing information and rejecting the obvious, and connecting opposing elements.

First, using an analogy helps you reconsider the elements of a problem in a different light, thus ensuring that you attempt to tackle it using fresh solutions.

Say your original problem is how to get more customers to buy a particular lipstick shade that's behind in the sales. To find a fresh approach, consider the problem in terms of an analogy: getting women to buy this lipstick shade is like getting children to try a new food item. How would you go about persuading children to eat something that's new to their eyes? Maybe give it a fun name or serve it wrapped in colorful trappings. From that analogy, you may then adapt the solutions to your original problem, such as giving the lipstick a fancy new name or attractive packaging.

Secondly, reversing information and rejecting the obvious are techniques that push you toward innovations and alternative paths by having you break the expected order of things.

For instance, the natural pattern for recharging mobile phones is that people need to go to a power source and plug in their phones there. Reversing this order has led to the development of a widely-used innovation: have the power source go with the person instead in the form of a wireless, portable power bank. Alternatively, you may reject the obvious. For example, consider how a phone might be recharged if it doesn't have sockets for charging wires. The result? Wireless charging pads on which phones may just be placed without a need for connecting wires.

And thirdly, connecting opposing elements is about taking random and opposing items and juxtaposing or linking them in some way—say, a snail on a skateboard, the sun carrying an umbrella, or a banana mopping the floor. This technique gives rise to interesting combinations and connections that breed fresh, creative ideas. For example, the snail on a skateboard may inspire a logo or ad on Internet speed boosters.

In addition, author Shane Snow suggests another lateral thinking technique called verbalizing the convention. This is about first identifying the conventional solution— i.e., how a typical person would solve the problem—and then asking yourself, "What if I couldn't take that route?" This forces you to think beyond the obvious solution.

Say the problem is about packing a travel bag that doesn't go beyond airline luggage weight limits. The obvious solution is to put the bag on a weighing scale. But what if there's no weighing scale? How would you solve the problem then?

It is by thinking laterally that breakthroughs and revolutionary ideas are born. By allowing you to see what've been called "rules" as merely conventions instead of absolutes, lateral thinking takes you to the threshold of great inventions and groundbreaking solutions. This has been the mechanism behind many of the innovations that have made their mark in history—from Picasso's cubism that broke the "rules" of proportion and perspective to Apple's tech revolution that aimed to simplify rather than submit to the conventional view that more buttons and more jargon meant better. And now that you know a number of techniques to hone and apply lateral thinking as well, you might just be the one to come up with the next big thing in your field as well.

Six hats method. Another useful concept from Edward de Bono of the previous section concerns the types of perspectives we can use. We've all heard the term that you must wear more than one hat, and as you might have guessed, it requires looking at a problem or decision from six separate perspectives by wearing six different hats.

Along with the hats themselves, an avatar that embodies the main purpose of each hat will make matters much clearer. It's like you are making a decision by committee, but all the roles are played by you. This is essentially the opposite of thinking with your instincts—you are making sure to uncover all pieces of relevant information and leave no stone unturned.

The colors of the six hats are white, red, black, yellow, green, and blue. The colors are fairly inconsequential, and it's probably easier if you categorize them by the avatar. I'll go into each of them in depth.

"Tell me more. What does this mean, and where did you get that information?"

The white hat is Sherlock Holmes, of course. This is the thinking and analytical hat. You are trying to gather as much information as possible by whatever means possible. Be observant and act like an information sponge. While you're at it, analyze your information and determine the gaps you have and what you can deduce from what you currently have. Dig deep, fill in the information gaps, and try to gather an understanding of what you really have in front of you.

You want to absorb as much of the available information as you can while also determining what you are missing to make a more informed and more perfect decision. The white hat is also where you should be resourceful about learning. As we discussed earlier, lack of information is one of the worst detriments to your decisions.

Make sure you are armed with information and you seek multiple perspectives and not let yourself be influenced by bias. You want an objective view of the entire landscape.

Get out your magnifying glass and start sleuthing, Detective Holmes.

"And how does that make you feel? Why is that?"

The red hat is Sigmund Freud, the psychotherapist. This is your emotion hat. You are trying to determine how you feel about something and what your gut tells you. Those are not always the same emotions. Combined with the information you collected as Sherlock Holmes, this will already give you a more complete picture than you are used to.

You are asking how you feel about your options and why. Beyond the objective level, decisions affect us on an emotional level. You must account for that—happiness and unhappiness. Ask yourself what you find yourself leaning toward or avoiding and why that might be. You can also attempt to predict how others might react emotionally.

Your actions might have consequences beyond your current understanding, and how people will feel is often different from how you think they will feel. What are the origins of your emotions toward each option, and are they reasonable or even relevant, for that matter? Often, our emotions aren't in the open, so when you can understand them better, you will understand your options better.

"I don't know. I have my doubts. What about X? Will Y really happen that way?"

The black hat is Eeyore, the morose donkey from *Winnie the Pooh*. If you don't know who that is, you can imagine the black hat to be the ultimate depressed pessimist that never believes anything will work out. Indeed, the purpose of the black hat is to attempt to poke holes in everything and to try to account for everything that can go wrong. They are skeptics who always look on the darker side of life.

They believe in *Murphy's law*: everything that can go wrong *will* go wrong. This is a hat most people never wear because they are afraid to look at their decisions, or reasoning, from a critical point of view. On some level, it probably indicates recognition that their views fall apart under deeper scrutiny, but that is exactly why it's so important to wear the black hat.

It's essentially planning for failure and the worst-case scenario. Planning for success is easy and instantaneous, but what happens when things don't work out and you have to put out fires? How would you plan differently if you thought there was a high probability of failure?

You change your approach, look for alternatives, and create contingency plans to account for everything. This is the type of analysis that leads to better planning and decisions because you can objectively take into account what is good and what is not. Wearing your black hat makes your plans tougher and stronger over the long haul, though it can be exhausting to continually reject positivity and hopefulness.

"It's going to be so great when this all comes together. Just imagine how you'll feel."

The yellow hat is the cheerleader. It is the opposite of the black hat—you are now thinking positively and optimistically. This is a motivating hat that allows you to feel good about your decision and the value of putting all the work into it. This is where you turn dark clouds into a silver lining.

It also allows you to project into the future and imagine the opportunities that come along with it. If this decision goes well, what else will follow? Where do optimistic projections place you, and what is necessary for you to reach them?

Belief in yourself is still one of the concepts that fuels achievement and motivation, so it's important to be balanced with pessimism and nitpicking flaws.

"Call me crazy, but what if we completely change X and try Y?"

The green hat is Pablo Picasso, the famous artist. This hat is for creativity. When you wear this hat, you want to think outside the box and come up with creative perspectives, angles, and solutions to whatever you are facing. It can be as simple as pretending that your current leading option is unavailable and having to figure out what you can do instead. You have to deviate from the current options and discover other ways of solving your problem.

Brainstorming is the name of the game here. No judgment or criticism is allowed when you are wearing this hat because you want to generate as many ideas as possible. You can always curate them later, but the more solutions you can think of, no matter how zany or ineffective, there will always be something you can learn or apply from them.

This is also a hat of open-mindedness and not being stuck in one track of thinking, which can be dangerous if you refuse to alter your course in the face of hardships.

"Now, now, children. Everyone will have their turn to be heard."

The blue hat is Henry Ford, founder of Ford Motor Company and inventor of the modern assembly line. The blue hat is all about coordinating and creating a system to integrate all the information you obtained from the other hats. You can also look at this hat as the CEO hat: you are in charge of making things happen and putting things in place, though not necessarily in charge of creating anything by yourself.

You are in charge of weighing how heavily each hat should be considered and what factors you must take into account when integrating the information. The CEO knows the context the best, so the input from each different hat is synthesized and weighed based on personal priorities and the situation at hand. You are the ultimate decider.

In summary, shifting your perspective is an important aspect of the problem-solving process, especially when you're faced with a complex problem for which traditional views and thinking styles just don't cut it anymore. When you need creative solutions for highly challenging or unconventional scenarios, you can count on several perspective-shifting techniques to help you through.

First, you may redefine problems through a number of ways: inversion or reverse brainstorming, paraphrasing, redirecting focus, varying the stress pattern, and substituting explicit definitions for terms in the problem statement. Second, you may engage in hypothetical thinking, challenging your mind to tackle "what if" questions to drive you toward innovative answers.

Finally, you may choose a more radical approach and take an entirely different viewpoint by seeing the problem from a psychological distance, tapping a combination of disciplines, lateral thinking, or using the six hats method. The variety of perspectives these strategies can help you take as you ponder on the problem is bound to lead you toward the most creative of ideas and the most ingenious of solutions.

Takeaways:

- Solving a problem will rarely occur if you stare at something long enough. After all, someone once said that engaging in the same act time after time and expecting a different outcome is insanity, right? For the record, it wasn't Einstein who said that often misattributed quote.
- Thus, we come to the solution that we must shift our perspectives to solve problems and think more effectively. We can invert problems, paraphrase and rephrase, vary the stress pattern, and substitute.
- We can also use a tried and true method of asking hypothetical questions. These are particularly effective because they allow you to pretend what your solution would be when elements of the problem appear or disappear one by one. Einstein was known for his use of thought experiments, which are just hypothetical

questions taken to the extreme and tested against reality. In fact, this is how he discovered that physics may not conform to Newton's three laws in every circumstance.

- Psychological distance helps in shifting your perspective because often our emotional investment clouds our judgment. As does lateral thinking, which asks us to use an analogy, reverse information and reject the obvious, and connect opposing elements.
- Finally, we come to the six hats method, which is a method designed exactly to make you think through six different perspectives. The easiest method to conceptualize these hats is through avatars: Sherlock Holmes (of course!), Sigmund Freud, Eeyore the donkey, a cheerleader, Pablo Picasso, and Henry Ford. Chances are that's five more perspectives than you would have had otherwise.

Chapter 5. Think Critically

Thinking critically is probably something you've heard of before, but it isn't clear from the name what it consists of.

Here's an easy definition: it's how to logically and rationally think about what's in front of you and getting a true and deep understanding about a subject. It's a type of thinking that allows you to solve problems easier, just because you are asking the right questions and determining what really matters. It accurately acknowledges that the information you need to make any type of decision will never be completely transparent and that you'll often have to go hunting for it. Therefore, it allows you to bypass your emotional decisions and reasoning and overall just think smarter.

It can be as simple as asking "why" five times in a row when you previously would've only asked once and stayed on the surface—or not have asked at all.

Why am I so unproductive at work? Because I have too much on my plate.

Why do you have so much on your plate? Because I keep getting tasks added onto it daily.

Why are you getting so many tasks added daily? Because I am the only one who can help.

Why are you the only one who can help? Because no one else has been trained, and our training systems are shoddy at best.

Why are our training systems so bad? Because our head trainer recently retired and no one has replaced him.

This is an elementary way of thinking about critical thinking, but you can immediately see the value in solving problems like Sherlock Holmes. At each stage of this critical thinking "why" chain, a different problem and solution appears to rear its head. It was first about you being unproductive and lazy, but then it became clear that it was a systemic problem. If you had stopped before reaching the next level, you wouldn't have been able to determine the cause of the problem and thus how to address it adequately. We could probably continue the "why" chain for a few more iterations, as well.

The solution we seek is not always plainly visible, and we might not even be addressing the correct problem. That's what critical thinking helps us with.

Though you should be open-minded and also humble, you should also learn to question what's in front of you. Not everything is what it seems. Critical thinking means not simply accepting information at face value. Information has a source, has a purpose, and has consequences—this is a level of analysis you are likely ignoring.

Critical thinking is the ability to think clearly and rationally about what to do or what to believe. It includes the ability to engage in reflective and independent thinking. Someone with critical thinking skills can do the following:

- understand the connections between ideas
- identify, construct, and evaluate arguments
- detect inconsistencies and mistakes in reasoning
- solve problems systematically
- identify the relevance and importance of ideas

Critical thinking is not a matter of accumulating information. A person with a good memory and who knows a lot of facts is not necessarily good at critical thinking. A critical thinker is able to deduce consequences from what he knows, and he knows how to make use of information to solve problems and to seek relevant sources of information to inform himself.

Critical thinking should also not be confused with being argumentative or being critical of other people. Although critical thinking skills can be used to expose fallacies and bad reasoning, critical thinking can also play an important role in cooperative reasoning and constructive tasks. Critical thinking can help us acquire knowledge, improve our theories, and strengthen arguments. We can use critical thinking to enhance work processes and improve social institutions.

The essence of critical thinking centers not on answering questions but on questioning answers, so it involves questioning, probing, analyzing, and evaluating. What follows are some of the most important and powerful aspects of critical thinking.

You may not need to do this with everything that comes your way, but training this habit and mindset will serve you well. For instance, when you travel to some countries, you inevitably know there are people that will try to scam you for your money. Critical thinking is the tool that protects you from these people.

Don't take anything at face value. The first step to thinking critically is to learn to evaluate what you hear, what you read, and what you decide to do. So rather than doing something because it's what you've always done or accepting what you've heard as the truth, spend some time just thinking. What's the problem? What are the possible solutions? What are the pros and cons of each? Of course, you still have to decide what to believe and what to do, but if you really evaluate things, you're likely to make a better, more reasoned choice.

Similarly, consider the source of information. Do they have their own biases or motives? What are their perspectives, and why might that be? Where information comes from is a key part of thinking critically about it. Everyone has a reason for what they say and do, and they might not even be aware of it. But it's up to you to find it.

Do your own research. All the information that gets thrown at us on a daily basis can be overwhelming, but if you decide to take matters into your own hands, it can also be a very powerful tool. If you have a problem to solve, a decision to make, or a perspective to evaluate, get onto Google and start reading about it. The more information you have, the better prepared you'll be to think things through and come up with a reasonable perspective or opinion. Don't rely on one person, because you never know what that person has relied upon. A singular view of an issue is destined to be biased.

Seek out assumptions. Most statements or assertions are based on certain assumptions. Sometimes these assumptions are explicit but are not always easy to find. For instance, a political opinion poll may well assume that voters in all constituencies and supporters of all political parties are equally likely to vote. This assumption may well be in the small print of the report if one looks hard enough. Sometimes assumptions may be implicit and therefore harder to discern. For instance, a political opinion poll may assume that everyone polled is telling the truth about their likely voting intentions. This sort of assumption is unlikely to be spelled out anywhere in a report.

Similarly, question assumptions that are explicit or unconscious. For instance, are voters in all constituencies and supporters of all political parties equally likely to vote? Maybe voters in affluent constituencies or supporters of political parties in opposition are more likely to vote. Or does everyone polled tell the truth about their likely voting intentions? Maybe supporters of racist parties are reluctant to be honest about their true voting intentions.

Don't assume you're right. I know it's hard. I struggle with the stubborn desire to be right as much as the next person— because being right feels awesome. It's an ego trip almost everyone aims to take at some point or another. But assuming you're right will often put you on the wrong track when it comes to thinking critically. If you don't take in other perspectives and points of view, think them over, and compare them to your own, you really aren't doing much thinking at all—and certainly not thinking of the critical kind.

This is related to *confirmation bias*. This is when we only seek out evidence to support our own stances or opinions. We are inclined to take more notice of, and give more weight to, evidence that appears to confirm our current opinion or judgment. Conversely, we tend to neglect or reject evidence that challenges our current position or stance.

Try to weigh the evidence impartially and follow the evidence wherever it takes you. It is so tempting to seize on evidence that confirms one's original view or the prevailing orthodoxy and to dismiss evidence that challenges it, but one needs to be open-minded about all the evidence and equally rigorous about establishing its authenticity.

Don't jump to conclusions. Although the currently available facts may suggest a particular conclusion, other conclusions may be possible. You're doing yourself a disservice if you stop prematurely at the first thing that appears to be acceptable. It's like stopping and spending all your money at the first shop you see in a mall. Further facts may support an alternative conclusion and even invalidate the original conclusion. Even when this is not the case, it is always helpful to have further, evidence to support the original conclusion. Continue asking questions and considering alternative explanations.

Whatever the case, you are almost always working with incomplete or bad information. Any conclusion you make is going to be a leap, but you can make sure it is a smaller leap rather than a bigger one.

Think about cause and effect. Correlation does not necessarily mean causation—that is, two variables often occurring together does not necessarily mean that one variable actually causes the other.

To take an easy example, when I get up from bed, the sun comes up—but there is obviously no causality. Yet some native tribes used to believe that particular rituals were essential to ensure the rising of the sun. A pattern was noticed and thus a relationship was assumed. In critical thinking, you should think about cause and effect, relationships, patterns, and what might be true if something else is true. These are known as inferences and deductions—Sherlock's specialties!

A deduction is where you take several statements or facts and say, "You said you went to medical school, work in a hospital, and saw a person you referred to as a 'patient.' I deduce that you are a doctor." It's an educated guess that's probably correct. An inference is less concrete. "You said you were a doctor. From that I infer that you're intelligent, care about people, and work in a hospital."

Think of a deduction as taking a lot of information and distilling it down to one fact. An inference is the opposite: you take one fact and extrapolate it out into several inferences. Deduction is a conclusion that is required by a premise and can be shown to be logically necessary if the premise is true. Inference is starting with a conclusion and then guessing a premise that would produce that conclusion as a necessary consequence if the premise is true.

Critical thinking will allow you to act like Sherlock in your life and understand what's happening around you. Your learning will go to the next level because you'll have a thorough view of any issue or information. I hope it is clear why mindsets are so important. You can call it being skeptical, critical, or just being suspicious about everything at first glance.

To be honest, these aren't bad policies to live by. You don't necessarily need to stop trusting everyone or anything, but you should get into the habit of understanding that not everything is as it seems. This is a major element of problem-solving and thinking creatively like Sherlock Holmes.

The Astronaut Method

Having the model of a process is always beneficial, and there's a sequence that can help you think more critically and thoughtfully. It comes from outer space.

Gene Kranz was a director for the Apollo 13 moon mission in 1970, which was aborted after an oxygen tank explosion occurred as the lunar module approached the moon. Apollo 13 is credited as a "successful failure," as NASA teams on earth effectively rescued the three pilots aboard the spacecraft.

Kranz's motto was "Failure is not an option." This was especially the case with the effort to save the astronauts, who were literally in a life-or-death situation. Surely some on the ground must have shared the astronauts' panic. But Kranz knew fear and distress weren't going to save the lives of the pilots. What was needed was a rational, thought-out, step-by-step process to cut through the anxiety and get everyone back home.

Thankfully, Kranz had such a process put in place. After a fire on a launch pad in 1967, he established a set of operational procedures to ensure that NASA crew members would logically and productively solve problems as they came up. It was critical thinking at its best and most methodical.

In the case of Apollo 13, Kranz's method worked. Instead of being remembered as a horrific tragedy or even just a disappointing flop, Apollo 13 is now described as a heroic American event. Kranz's process is hailed as a classic model of how to mindfully and patiently work through problems using critical analysis, assessment, and thinking—not "making things worse by guessing."

If the astronaut method was successful in saving the lives of three men 200,000 miles away from earth, then imagine how it can work on the less consequential—but still difficult—problems we have here at home.

How does the astronaut method work? Let's look at the steps. There are eight of them.

1. Define the problem. When something goes wrong, there's often a flush of panic and dread. That's a reasonable reaction, but it contributes nothing to a possible solution. Instead, the first thing that's needed is to determine the exact nature of the problem that faces you.

This is a vital first step because it establishes a tone of rationality right off the bat. An objective, reasonable description of the crisis helps to cut through the alarm and terror and start the neutral, moderated problem-solving process.

For example, let's choose a common problem that, while not necessarily a fatal or life-threatening situation, sure bugs everyone now and then: not having a lot of money.

The problem is that, after you've paid your bills and bought what you need, you don't have much left over. You can't save money or do anything fun because there's nothing left in your budget. That's your problem—it can be defined as simply as that.

2. Determine goals and objectives. This should be a fairly more complex answer than "Uh... you know, *fixing the problem*?"

Now that you've identified what the issue is, what are the specific aspects of the problem that you need to repair or adjust? How will the situation look like as soon as the problem is solved? And what favorable result will solving this problem bring about?

In our example, your goals and objectives are more than just "having more money." Sure, that's the starting point, but what do you want to happen once you get your money? You might want to have a financial nest egg for the future. Or you might want to be able to afford a new home entertainment system or go on an enjoyable holiday.

3. Generate an array of alternative solutions. This is a brainstorming exercise and the point in this process to really "think outside the box." Considering the problem and the goals, come up with a wide range of potential ways to fix or remedy the situation. They can be simple, one-step solutions and more elaborate ones (ideally both). They can be relatively easy or more ambitious. What's important is to produce as many options as you can. As we saw earlier with the Osborn-Parnes model, most of us are only starting at this stage without considering the first two steps. This can have detrimental effects.

For our example, you can come up with a range of solutions like this:

A. Just spend more money on what you want.

B. Work more.

C. Prioritize parts of your lifestyle so you spend less money.

D. Ask someone for a loan.

We'll stop at four potential solutions for this problem—but in practice, generate as many as you can think of, whether it's four or 14.

4. Evaluate the possible consequences of each solution. For all the answers you've just come up with, what are the most likely outcomes? Determine what risks each solution will entail, the best- and worst-case scenarios that could result, and a more realistic theory about how these solutions may impact the future.

Let's apply this step to our example. For each of those potential solutions above, these are potential outcomes:

A. *Just spend more money*: You might feel a temporary sense of relief and happiness if you just go for the gusto and throw money where you need to—but if it's all you do, you run the risk of getting further into debt and losing what you have now.

B. *Work more*: You'll get more cash flow coming in. But you may lose a lot of valuable time you need for other things in your life. You might not get that much more money to make it worthwhile. And besides, there may not be enough extra work for you to do anyway.

C. *Prioritize your spending*: In this scenario you might have to make hard choices. You could suspend a couple of things you do now that you really enjoy. On the other hand, you might get a better grip on your finances, realize some cuts you make won't bother you that much, and save a little more.

D. *Ask someone for a loan*: You'll get an influx of new money if you ask a relative or friend to lend you some. But then that'll just become another financial debt for you, and if the loan goes unpaid for a long time, it might cause a strain on your relationship.

5. Use this analysis to choose one (or more) course of action. After considering all the angles of all the potential solutions you've thought up, make a very informed choice which one you'll execute.

If you're lucky enough to have a rather obvious single answer, that's great. If a few solutions look like strong answers to the problem, you can choose as many of them as you want (though it's best to have a limited number). You'll need to choose one to work on exclusively for the rest of this process, but you can keep the others as backup plans. There's nothing wrong with having solid Plan B's.

For our example, after you've carefully considered each of your options, you've settled on one that seems like it might be the most reasonable: Option C, reorganizing your spending priorities. That's the solution you decide to execute. Option B (working more) is your next-best solution, so keep that in mind as a fallback. But until the end of this process, just concentrate on getting Option C in action.

6. Plan the implementation. This is a crucial step that, given a reasonable about of time, shouldn't be skipped or hurried through. Make an organized outline that details how you will execute the solution. List the steps, what resources you need to carry out the plan, where and when each step will be implemented, and who will be responsible for each step if there are multiple people involved.

To execute the option in our example, you'd gather data on your spending habits and where all the money goes (receipts, bank statements, spreadsheets, etc.). You'd review it against how much income you typically get in a certain amount of time. You'd draw up a new spreadsheet and itemize your expenses into amounts that are unchangeable (rent or car payments, utilities, cell phone), bills you might have some flexibility in repaying (credit card), and amounts you have total control over (food, clothing, entertainment).

You decide to make some changes in that last category. You'll pare back on your entertainment budget and spend more leisure time at home. You'll cut back on buying new clothes (or learn to love the thrift shop). You plan to spend less money on eating out by going grocery shopping and cooking at home. (Don't know how to cook? You have the Internet, which has an endless supply of cooking lessons. Not only are you planning a solution, but you're planning to learn a new skill as well. Thank you, budget process!) As people say, ideas are a dime a dozen, but execution is rare.

7. Implement with full commitment. Now it's time to set the plan in motion—and not look back until it's finished. That's the important part. Any misgivings you might have had should have been addressed in Steps 4 and 5. So now that the solution's been chosen and implemented, launch and let it run its course. You'll have time for assessment afterward if the solution fails. But for now, get it going and support it totally.

For our example, you may have set a date to start the process. When that date comes, bam—you put it into play. You've planned everything, so you know what you can expect. You won't spend a lot of time clothes shopping and you'll miss it a little bit. You might miss a couple of big movies you were looking forward to. But you power through it. Besides, you just saw a video on YouTube about how to make lasagna for less than $2 per serving and you're eager to try it out. Boil that pasta and don't look back.

8. Adapt as needed based on incoming data. Hopefully, in Step 6, you planned how you'll evaluate the success of the solution as it happens. So as you observe the process and review that information, make changes or tweaks that will improve operation and increase the chance of success. Maybe your solution's working well and there aren't many changes required. Maybe (but improbably) everything's going perfectly and you don't need *any* changes. Whatever the case, it's essential that you get data as the process is running and that you review it objectively and critically.

In our example, after a couple of months of putting your budget into practice, you see great improvement. You've cut back on a lot of spending, you're saving some money, and you've realized you didn't need a lot of what you bought anyway. You're being more creative about what to do in your leisure time, and that feels great too. And to top it all off, now you can make chicken Parmesan. However, some of your suits or outfits are falling apart, so you're going to tweak your clothing budget a little bit.

And there you go. You've put a new plan into action, it's working, and you're monitoring it. You're running a monthly budget just like the astronauts do!

Takeaways:

- Thinking critically is more than being critical and negative. It's accepting that what you see is only the tip of the iceberg and that there is always more than meets the eye. Critical thinking is the process you use to find out what lies beneath.

- The simplest way of critical thinking is to ask questions, interrogate, and create a "why" chain. At each step of a "why" chain, a different problem and solution appears. Eventually, if you go deep enough, you'll find the lead domino that is the true problem you need to solve.

- Critical thinking also consists of specific thinking patterns to get into the habit of. These include questioning and finding assumptions, resisting jumping to conclusions, searching for cause and effect, and asking "If this is true, what else is true?"

- A specific methodology that combines critical thinking and problem-solving is called the astronaut method, which has eight steps: define the problem, determine goals and objectives, generate a list of solutions, evaluate possible consequences, evaluate and choose a course of action, plan the implementation, commit fully, and adapt to new information after the fact.

Summary Guide

Chapter 1. Think Like Sherlock Holmes

- Can you think like Sherlock? Yes and no. Let's take a brief jaunt through Sherlock's bibliography to understand this answer.

- Sherlock is an expert in just about every discipline that is in or adjacent to criminal justice. This includes handwriting analysis (at a time when this was more legitimate and relevant), codebreaking, and much more. Sherlock also boasts a photographic memory and the ability to read people like a master FBI interrogator.

- Of course we can't demonstrate these traits to the same degree as Sherlock Holmes, but we can improve the traits that help us solve problems. We can learn to observe and make deductions, we can increase our knowledge in relevant disciplines, and we can also improve our memories. In general, we can learn to think more creatively to generate solutions, which might not be on Sherlock's level but are helpful anyway.

Chapter 2. Thinking Outside The Box

- Thinking outside the box is how you can attack a problem or situation from different angles. Staring at a problem through the same lens will rarely yield results, so it's typically necessary to engage in ways that are entirely foreign to you. You are expanding your set of mental tools in this chapter.

- SCAMPER is a tool for creative thinking, as it provides seven distinct ways of approaching a problem: (S) substitute, (C) combine, (A) adapt, (M) minimize/magnify, (P) put to another use, (E) eliminate, and (R) reverse.

- The Osborn-Parnes model is typically known as the creative problem-solving method. It consists of a few steps as well, though most of us start from step four because this Osborn-Parnes model deals with situations where you're not sure what the problem even is: (1) mess-finding, (2) fact-finding, (3) problem-finding, (4) idea-finding, (5) solution-finding, and (6) action-finding or acceptance-finding.

- Creating intentional constraints can force creativity because they require innovation to make something work. There are numerous examples provided, such as dealing with copyright violations, but it can be as simple as asking "What if we had to do things in this certain way?"
- Altered states of consciousness have been shown to contribute to creativity. This occurs specifically with regards to sleepiness and daydreaming. When you are sleepy, what are known as theta waves are released in spades, and these aid creativity. Salvador Dali was known to take advantage of this so-called hypnagogic phase of sleep by falling asleep holding a key over a plate, so

when he fell asleep, the key would fall and the ensuing noise would wake him up. Daydreaming takes advantage of the fact that when we are in that state, we tend to engage in divergent thinking versus convergent thinking.

- Finally, combinatory play, as popularized by Albert Einstein, is not simply about playing and distracting oneself from the task at hand. Actually, it's about the startling unoriginality of creativity. Everything is derivative, inspired by something else, and otherwise interrelated. Thus, when you engage in combinatory play, you are taking elements from extremely different disciplines and mashing them together subconsciously.

Chapter 3. Observations and Deductive Reasoning

- A key element of Sherlock's problem-solving abilities is the ability to use information—specifically, taking in and absorbing information and then connecting the dots and making deductions and hypotheses based on that information. We all look at the same situations, yet some of us come away with completely different conclusions. That's because of what is done with the information in (1) observations and (2) deductions.

- Observations are all about taking in information. The truth is, we really aren't very observant in our daily lives. You probably don't know the color of the ceiling or floor in the room you are currently in. Becoming better at observations helps your problem-solving because that's where your solutions will come from.

- You can focus on becoming more detail-oriented, devoting 100% of your focus and attention, paying attention to the baseline of people and situations, understanding people's self-perceptions, and taking a look at the big picture and not getting lost in the details.

- Deductions are about connecting the dots and explaining what's in front of you. Deductions are essentially storytelling in reverse. You can accomplish this by learning the fishbone method of naming causes and motivations, training yourself to think through cause and effect, watching people and trying to assign a narrative or story to an interaction, talking out loud, and putting ego aside to allow yourself to explore solutions and reasons that are against your beliefs.

Chapter 4. Shift Your Perspective

- Solving a problem will rarely occur if you stare at something long enough. After all, someone once said that engaging in the same act time after time and expecting a different outcome is insanity, right? For the record, it wasn't Einstein who said that often misattributed quote.
- Thus, we come to the solution that we must shift our perspectives to solve problems and think more effectively. We can invert problems, paraphrase and rephrase, vary the stress pattern, and substitute.

- We can also use a tried and true method of asking hypothetical questions. These are particularly effective because they allow you to pretend what your solution would be when elements of the problem appear or disappear one by one. Einstein was known for his use of thought experiments, which are just hypothetical questions taken to the extreme and tested against reality. In fact, this is how he discovered that physics may not conform to Newton's three laws in every circumstance.

- Psychological distance helps in shifting your perspective because often our emotional investment clouds our judgment. As does lateral thinking, which asks us to use an analogy, reverse information and reject the obvious, and connect opposing elements.

- Finally, we come to the six hats method, which is a method designed exactly to make you think through six different perspectives. The easiest method to conceptualize these hats is through avatars: Sherlock Holmes (of course!), Sigmund Freud, Eeyore the donkey, a cheerleader, Pablo Picasso, and Henry Ford. Chances are that's five more perspectives than you would have had otherwise.

Chapter 5. Think Critically

- Thinking critically is more than being critical and negative. It's accepting that what you see is only the tip of the iceberg and that there is always more than meets the eye. Critical thinking is the process you use to find out what lies beneath.

- The simplest way of critical thinking is to ask questions, interrogate, and create a "why" chain. At each step of a "why" chain, a different problem and solution appears. Eventually, if you go deep enough, you'll find the lead domino that is the true problem you need to solve.

- Critical thinking also consists of specific thinking patterns to get into the habit of. These include questioning and finding assumptions, resisting jumping to conclusions, searching for cause and effect, and asking "If this is true, what else is true?"

- A specific methodology that combines critical thinking and problem-solving is called the astronaut method, which has eight steps: define the problem, determine goals and objectives, generate a list of solutions, evaluate possible consequences, evaluate and choose a course of action, plan the implementation, commit fully, and adapt to new information after the fact.

Printed in Great Britain
by Amazon

53817615R00131